WALKING WITH MURDER

To Grace

who has shared our
home and world travels
with David Balfour
Allan Breck and
Robert Louis Stevenson

Walking with Murder

On the *Kidnapped* Trail

Ian Nimmo

Birlinn

First published in Great Britain in 2005 by
Birlinn Ltd
West Newington House
10 Newington Road
Edinburgh
EH9 1QS

www.birlinn.co.uk

ISBN 10: 1 84158 409 6

ISBN 13: 978 1 84158 409 6

British Library Cataloguing-in-Publication Data
A catalogue record for this book is available
on request from the British Library

Typeset by Carnegie Publishing, Lancaster
Printed and bound by The Cromwell Press, Trowbridge, Wiltshire

Contents

FIGURE I. Flashback: A youthful Ian Nimmo on the *Kidnapped* trail in 1960.

Preface

Robert Louis Stevenson, his essays, poems and novels have been passions of mine for as long as I can remember. My childhood and youth were spent in the Highlands and therefore *Kidnapped* in particular perhaps had a special appeal. As the years passed, I became intrigued with the Appin Murder, the mystery of who shot the 'Red Fox', the hanging of a man I believed to be innocent, the secret name of the real murderer, and Stevenson's skill in weaving his fiction into the fact. In 1960 I pulled on my climbing boots, heaved up my rucksack and headed for the tiny island of Erraid off the most westerly point of the Ross of Mull where David Balfour, the hero of *Kidnapped*, was shipwrecked. Erraid was my starting point to follow in the footsteps of David and the Jacobite fugitive, Allan Breck Stewart, all the way back to Edinburgh. It now means, of course, that off and on for more than four decades I have been gathering material for this book. I have now tramped the *Kidnapped* route twice, and made countless excursions to check facts and try out new theories along its length. All of it has been an enormous pleasure, but I have also witnessed with fascination – and sometimes dismay – the far-reaching changes that have taken place across the Highlands today, the movement of people, the challenge to the old order and culture that has put a language and way of life under further threat.

In the writing of this book, I have tried to keep a sensible approach to the spelling of place names, which have also changed over two-and-a-half centuries. Stevenson altered some spellings in *Kidnapped*, probably for writer reasons. For example, Allan Breck is spelled with one 'l' rather than two, most likely to draw the distinction between the fact and fiction. Contemporary documents of 1752, when the murder took place, spelled Allan with a double 'l' and so have I. It was probably also to emphasise the fictional account that Stevenson advanced the action by a year to 1751. Both Ardshiel, captain of the

Appin Regiment, and his home, now a fine hotel, have taken different spellings over the years, and for consistency I have kept to the old spelling. Mountains, glens, lochs and villages are in accordance with the Ordnance Survey to ease the way for those who try to follow the *Kidnapped* trail today. Where Stevenson departs from the historical facts for the sake of his story I have mostly drawn attention to the change. David Balfour measured his march in miles, and miles have been good enough for me. It would ring false to count them in kilometres to reflect a period midway through the eighteenth century. Likewise, for consistency, I have given the heights of mountains in feet rather than metres.

The map which accompanied the early *Kidnapped* editions should be taken as a guide only. Although Stevenson provided detailed written instructions, discrepancies occurred between the text, the instructions and the route as it finally appeared from his cousin David A. Stevenson's drawing office in Edinburgh. *Kidnapped* was written in Bournemouth, and one of the difficulties may have been that Stevenson was working on a very small-scale map, references may have become misunderstood and the long lines of communication may not have helped. For example, in the *Kidnapped* text the Torosay ferry clearly deposits David Balfour going from Mull to Kinlochaline, at the head of Loch Aline. The original map suggests David landed further up the coast towards Fiunary and walked to Kinlochaline. There are several of these small discrepancies on the route and I have pointed them out where appropriate.

A great many people have been of help to me. It would be impossible now to name them all after such a long time, but I would particularly like to thank the following: the staffs of the National Library of Scotland, the Edinburgh Room of the Central Library, Edinburgh; the National Archives Scotland; the Writers' Museum, Edinburgh; the West Highland Museum, Fort William; members of the Appin Historical Society and the Mull Historical Society; Inverness Library; members of the Robert Louis Stevenson Club and especially Anne Gray and Elizabeth Warfel; the Public Record Office, London; the British Museum, London; members of the Stewart Society; Alastair Campbell of Airds; the late High Court judge Lord 'Jock' Cameron; the late Malcolm Thomson, former head of Edinburgh, Lothian and Borders CID; former detective-inspector Leslie Liney from Pitlochry;

Paul Johnston of the Findhorn Community on the island of Erraid; John Cameron and his wife Mary, of Knockvoligan, opposite Erraid; Joan Faithful; the late Alasdair 'Attie' MacKechnie from Fionnphort, Isle of Mull; the Rev Anne Winning at Lochaline; and Anne and Iain Cameron of Camas na Croise in Morvern. I would also like to thank all those former climbing and hillwalking friends from the old days – in particular Jim Seaton – who did part of the walk with me and gave me the benefit of their company and theories on the Appin Murder and the continuing mystery. I also pay tribute to the outstanding research into the Appin Murder carried out by Lt. General Sir William MacArthur, Seamus Carney and James Hunter in their books on the subject, and my thanks also to other writers who have touched on aspects of the Appin Murder in the past.

Ian Nimmo

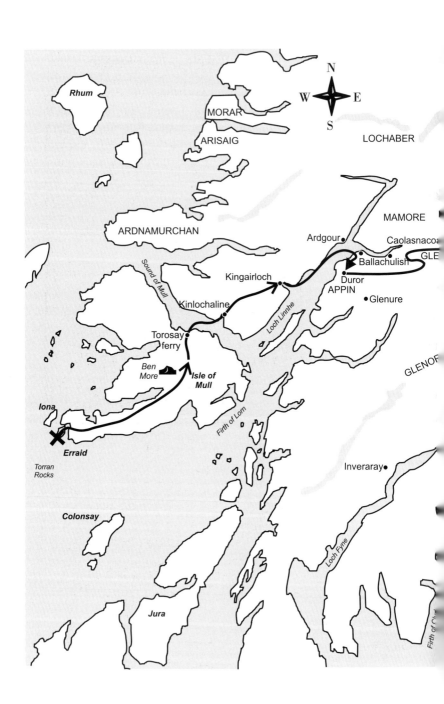

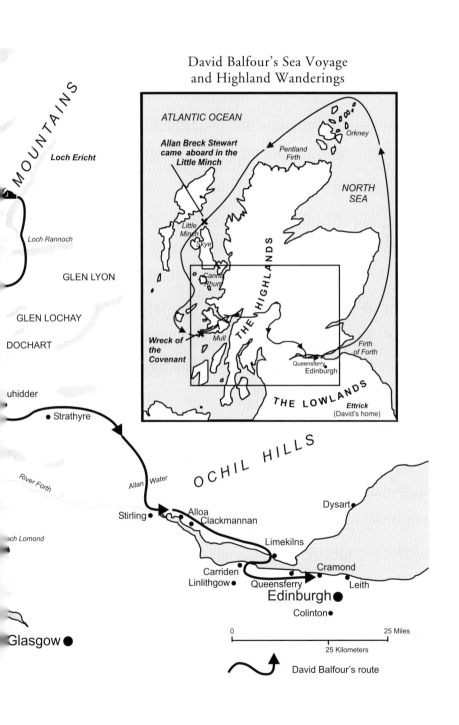

David Balfour's Sea Voyage
and Highland Wanderings

Illustrations

Introduction:
After Culloden

Six years after the 1745 Jacobite Uprising came to a bloody end at Culloden the scars from the Duke of Cumberland's ruthless 'peacemakers' remained livid. The house burnings and pillage on the forfeited Stewart estate of Appin in Argyll and the neighbouring Cameron country of Callart and Mamore might have ended, but the Hanoverian rule continued to be oppressive. Weapons and tartans were still proscribed. Jacobite resentment glared from every doorway.

To the victors after Culloden went the spoils. The vanquished were left with only pain, poverty and humiliation. Among the victors were the Campbells. They had remained firm to the Hanoverian cause and were now experiencing the benefits by taking over defeated clan lands. Clans, crown and government remained jittery.

For the government, further Jacobite rebellions lurked behind every bush; for the clans there was only a fading hope that they might rise again to end their distress. Crown insecurity was demonstrated by unnecessary harshness. The clans had nothing but their banned weapons buried under thatches or dug into hillsides ready for the day that never came.

Among the clansmen who escaped to France was Charles Stewart, captain of the Appin Regiment. Its ranks had been grimly thinned during that final battle, although the Appin colours, the yellow cross on the blue background, had fluttered bravely. Charles's family home was Ardshiel House, a fine mansion in an idyllic location by Kentallen. After Culloden, Ardshiel was hunted hard before reaching France. At his side throughout this harrowing period was local man and professional soldier, Allan Breck Stewart, a deserter from General 'Johnny' Cope's routed army at Prestonpans.

In the wake of Culloden, Ardshiel's house was partially dismantled, then partly burned after the timbers were sold to raise a few pounds for the Hanoverian government. Cattle were driven off, furnishings and belongings taken in the name of the law. Ardshiel's wife, Isabel, complained she was not even left a pot to cook for her family. It was winter, she was heavily pregnant, without roof or means of support, and the child of the Stewart chief of Appin was born in a nearby shed. The rest of the Stewarts watched their clan's plight helplessly – and smouldered.

The man appointed factor to both the Appin and Callart estates was red-headed Colin Campbell of Glenure. His task was to administer the farms, set and collect rents. But not only was Glenure dealing with defeated, embittered and poverty-stricken clansmen, he was innocently part of a feud between Stewarts and Campbells which spanned centuries. Glenure was unfortunate enough to represent a branch of the Campbells associated with the loss of Stewart lands in Lorne some three hundred years previously. Memories were long and clan grudges were nursed. Now the Stewarts were seeing their beloved Appin taken over by their sworn enemies. Stewarts were being evicted from Stewart properties and Glenure's hated Campbell relatives installed in their place.

The man who spoke for the Stewarts in this fraught situation, and represented as best he could the interests of Isabel Stewart, was Ardshiel's half-brother James. In a land of many Stewarts with the same first name, James was known as Seumas a' Ghlinne, James of the Glen, for ease of identification. His glen was Glen Duror, where he farmed Achindarroch, a mile beyond Kentallen. James had served as a captain in the Appin Regiment and was in the thick of it at Culloden.

As the representative of a broken clan, James's task of trying to look after Stewart interests was thankless and hopeless. A wrong word, a misjudged reaction and the consequences could be dire from a vengeful government determined not to be challenged again by arms in the Highlands.

In what was a fearful situation, James was regarded as a man of ability, trusted by those who had dealings with him, a calm and honest man with deep religious convictions. He also had a sharp eye for a farming deal, and by astute management he had earlier turned his Achindarroch farm into a sound business, buying and selling the black cattle that were the main source of income in the area. When he saw the way the wind shifted as the Campbells took over, James vacated Achindarroch before he could be evicted. Campbell of Airds, a neighbour and long-standing friend, rented to him the Duror farm of Acharn.

Colin Campbell of Glenure had served as a lieutenant in Flanders with Loudoun's regiment, and gave a good enough account of himself, it was said. He had missed Culloden because his regiment had been disbanded, but he served in the Argyll Militia for a time without seeing action. Before his appointment as king's factor, he had been well settled in his Glenure estate, which he inherited from his father, Patrick Campbell of Glenure and Barcaldine. His elder brother, John, took over the larger Barcaldine interest. Colin Campbell's good humour, reasonableness, commonsense – and his courage – were qualities which equipped him to be as good a man as any to handle the mistrust, fear and resentment abroad in Appin and Callart.

Both Colin Campbell and James Stewart were men of calibre, but also incidental figures in the larger government game of taming the Highlands. They knew each other well enough. The small estate of Glenure was half-way up Glen Creran, a day's hike by the coast road from Duror, but a much shorter distance across country for a hillman. James and Red Colin worked together as well as could be expected in the circumstances; their association went back years and there had been some friendship.

It was not an easy situation for Glenure to manage. Such was the Hanoverian government's zeal against all clansmen that even Glenure himself as a Highlander was under suspicion. His lack of urgency in carrying out their harsh policies was being read as sympathy for the Jacobites. There could have been substance in these doubts, of course, for Glenure's mother was the daughter of a well-known Jacobite Cameron. In fact, Glenure was recognised locally as a decent, intelligent, able, loyal man, with a young wife, Janet MacKay, daughter of a Sutherland landowner. She was around 18 when she married Glenure, half his age, and now they had two small children.

Glenure was well aware of the earlier burning outrages visited upon his Appin neighbours. He did not wish to appear unreasonable or too heavy-handed in his dealings with the Stewart tenants in spite of his orders to the contrary. There were discussions with James, social visits, the bottle had been out and an uneasy but sensible working relationship was established. Glenure wisely recognised that the Stewarts would take instructions more readily from James than from himself and therefore Seumas a' Ghlinne became Glenure's sub-factor.

But Glenure was being pressured by his political masters and the money men of the Barons Exchequer in Edinburgh. It had been reported that laxity reigned in pursuing government objectives in the estates of Cameron of Lochiel, Cameron of Callart, the McDonals of Kinlochmoidart and Stewart of Ardshiel. Jacobites still remained in possession of these lands and most had been 'out' in the 'Forty-Five. This situation, it was demanded, must end forthwith. Suspicions about Glenure's loyalty to the crown gave him no leeway. His instructions had to be carried out in full. Tenants must pay their rents, take a voluntary oath of allegiance to the government – or they must go.

Inevitably, the Cameron and Stewart tenants resented paying rents to a government that treated them so harshly, and with such contempt, particularly when the rents were being collected by a Campbell. Inability to pay was a further argument. There was a compelling reason for this – in Appin they were already scraping together a clandestine rent to keep the exiled Ardshiel in reasonable comfort in France. James Stewart was also the collector of this rent.

In the clan system it was important that the position, dignity and wellbeing of the chief was maintained. Paying two rents could be interpreted as noble, but Isabel Stewart was also bringing threats to bear on the tenants to pay the clan levy. A reasonable second rent was expected by the tenants, but Isabel's demands became excessive. Loyalty could go only so far, and the hard-done-by Stewart tenants, harried for the official government rent on one hand and threatened by the wife of their clan captain for the clan rent on the other, took action against Lady Isabel and she was forced to return a portion.

Allan Breck Stewart was the go-between in all of this. His role was to transport the money to Ardshiel in France and act as a two-way messenger to Appin kinsmen on both sides of the water. Like a modern-day secret agent, Allan Breck was spirited in and out of the country, although how many times is not known. In Appin, where his life was forfeit if government troops laid hands on him, he was made welcome and strolled around freely.

It was the evictions that brought matters to a head. Warning notices were delivered to 'four or five' Appin tenants. They were not Stewarts, but they had been introduced by James and were prepared to pay an increased government rent, plus the Ardshiel 'second rent' as well as take the oath of loyalty demanded by the government. They had not done so previously because it had not been an issue.

The sheer unfairness of evicting these tenants in such circumstances infuriated James. Any friendship that existed between himself and Colin Campbell died at that time. Glenure, who had tried to be lenient from the outset, was now helpless. His instructions were clear-cut. Even then, to the last he demonstrated his sympathy by arranging that those who faced eviction could stay on and act as 'boumen' (managers for the new lairds). In this way they would still be able to earn a living. He could do no more.

James Stewart travelled to Edinburgh to try to harness the law on the tenants' behalf. As the evictions approached, in May, 1752, both Appin and Callart were in a state of high tension …

I

The Murder of Colin Campbell

There came a shot from a firelock from higher up the hill;
and with the very sound of it Glenure fell upon the road.
'Oh, I am dead!' he cried, several times over ...

The killing of the 'Red Fox', from
Robert Louis Stevenson's *Kidnapped*

Three of the figures were on horseback and the fourth on foot. They edged their way slowly along the rough road by the south shore of Loch Linnhe in Argyll. The one-eyed ferryman, Ewan Mackenzie, had set them down in the Stewart country of Appin from Callart on the other side of the loch. Their landing place was half-a-mile westwards from where the iron bridge now spans the narrows of Loch Leven near Ballachulish. It was late afternoon of a sunny May day and Appin looked its finest.

It is important to appreciate the imposing landscape, the grandeur and scale of the mountains all around, and their relationship with the deep-running sea lochs below, to understand why men would give their lives for such country. In summer, the high tops here can turn arctic in a trice, in winter the blizzards and ice walls are awesome and lethal. As the little group moved slowly towards Kentallen, the twin-peaked Beinn a' Bheithir heaved skywards on their left; behind them the distinctive stone nose of Sgorr na Ciche marked the end of the Aonach Eagach's rocky sawblade; towards Kinlochleven, Am Bodach and Nagruachan were still etched in white; and across the loch the tumbling Ardgour hills looked like blue thunder clouds.

Along Loch Linnhe side, in Appin's favoured climate at sea level, the birch trees, rowans and alders were displaying fresh leaves, new bracken was uncurling from last season's brown tangles and the spring-green grasses were just high enough to hide a man with murder on his mind. Herons fished the water's edge, oyster catchers, curlews and a variety of waders were finding rich pickings. The bobbing heads of seals, and occasionally otters, broke the surface as they do today. The sweet spring sounds of Appin were concentrated in the little wood of Lettermore at the height of the nesting season.

It was with relief that the tiny group stepped from the ferry into Appin. The crossing was a tedious business, with much rowing depending on wind and tide. Two of the group went over with the horses first, then the ferry returned to collect the others. The leader of the foursome, the big, bluff, red-headed Colin Campbell of Glenure, turned to his colleagues and commented, almost with a sense of deliverance: 'I'm safe now I'm out of my mother's country!'

With him were his 25-year-old Edinburgh lawyer nephew, Mungo Campbell; sheriff's officer Donald Kennedy (48), from Inveraray, who had come up to meet Glenure at Fort William with urgent legal papers; and Glenure's servant, the 19-year-old John Mackenzie.

Glenure was well enough known. Locally he was called Cailean Ruadh, or 'Red Colin'. His name was on the lips of everyone, and some spat as they said it. His every movement was monitored, often by unseen eyes. Rumours of Cameron plots against his life in Callart had been whispered for months. This was ambush country, and on several occasions Glenure felt the cold sweat rise on the small of his back as he anticipated a sniper's bullet. The young servant John Mackenzie had stayed close to Glenure all the way across Callart, placing himself between possible lines of fire and his master.

The whole area was in turmoil. Glenure had been appointed government factor to administer the Cameron country of Callart and Mamore as well as the Stewart estate of Ardshiel in Appin. These were forfeited clan lands after the failed 1745 Jacobite uprising. Part of Glenure's duties was to set and collect rents from the tenants. From the beginning, relationships had been barely tolerable. The Camerons in particular gave him such a hostile reception that he feared for his life.

In both Callart and Appin there were bitter arguments over the rents, then their backdating. The situation became inflamed by Campbells or their friends taking over Stewart properties. Finally, a small number of evictions were planned on all the estates. The disaffected tenants viewed the evictions as unjust and provocative. There was agitation, anger – and an increasing sense of premonition.

Glenure was well aware of the risks. It was therefore with courage that he went to Callart and Mamore to try to resolve some of these problems, but also to begin the evictions. As he saw it, the law was on his side and he had troops at his back if they were eventually needed. His eviction plans in Callart on the day were foiled, however, because the sheriff-depute did not turn up and it was important that the evictions were seen to be carried out in a proper, legal manner.

Glenure crossed into Appin with some frustration as well as relief. It had not gone well in Callart, he thought, but confrontation with the tenants was a duty postponed only 24 hours. Five evictions were to be actioned in Appin on the following day.

As that little group made its way along the side of Loch Linnhe, Colin Campbell met up with the respected and elderly Alexander Stewart of Ballachulish, a senior figure in Appin, whose house was only a short distance from the ferry. Showing courtesy to the older man, Glenure dismounted and the pair walked together for a time while the others moved ahead. In spite of the tension over the next day's evictions, the subject was avoided. Donald Kennedy, who was walking, had taken off his coat and given it to the young servant Mackenzie to carry on his saddle. The coat was dropped, the elder Ballachulish saw it and called to Mackenzie, who rode back to pick it up. Glenure parted with Ballachulish in friendship as they reached the Wood of Lettermore.

The road here rose above and away from the loch to avoid a cliff face. As they entered the wood, Donald Kennedy was leading the way, while Glenure and Mungo Campbell rode almost abreast at a slow walking pace until they came to a rough, narrow section, where Mungo moved ahead. John Mackenzie, delayed by retrieving the fallen coat, was now well to the rear.

As the old road began to flatten out, a steep bank was on their left, with another sheer rock face a little above and beyond. Glenure and Mungo were in deep conversation. The following day's evictions monopolised their thoughts. They were still in hostile territory, without weapons, only a short distance from their Kentallen destination, where they would spend the night. They felt the most dangerous part of their day was over. Their conversation was about

FIGURE 2. The plaque on the little cairn in the Wood of Lettermore where government agent Colin Campbell of Glenure – Stevenson's 'Red Fox' – was shot in the back by an unknown hand.

the evictions, tactics, possibilities, opportunities, a dram at the end of their journey – and almost certainly there would have been reference to that stunning Appin scenery all around.

Suddenly, a single shot rang from the hillside. At once Glenure slumped in the saddle. He called out: 'Oh, I am dead. He's going to shoot you. Take care of yourselves.' Or some such words.

Chaos followed. One shot had been fired, but two bullets had entered Glenure's back, exiting from his abdomen. He was bleeding profusely. Mungo helped his dying uncle from his horse and laid him on the ground. Soon Glenure was falling in and out of consciousness.

Kennedy and Mackenzie rushed to them, bending low, eyes on the hillside in case of further attack. They crouched, trying to make themselves smaller targets, expecting to come under further fire at any moment. Their eyes raked the steep hillside above. They spoke in whispers. Then Mungo told Mackenzie to make best speed on the fastest horse to Kentallen Inn to get help.

They were in shock. Perhaps that explains why Mungo's evidence at the subsequent trial became contradictory. Mungo declared he saw a man wearing a 'short dark coat' with a gun in his hand. It was at such a distance, however, that Mungo's first impression was that this figure could not have been the assassin. He took some steps up the hill to give chase, he recollected. Later, Mungo went back on this statement, but in his confusion he could not even remember whether he ran up the hill before or after attending to his dying uncle – and the exact timing of shot and sighting of suspect is critical evidence. The suspicion immediately arises that more than one person may have been involved. The others said they saw nothing.

It was the perfect spot for an ambush. Glenure's broad back high in the saddle, moving slowly and in clear vision, presented a simple shot. The hillside is steep there, but a bulge on its flank only 50 feet or so above the path blocks the view of the higher slopes. All the gunman had to do was reach the bulge and disappear. It would have taken him under 60 seconds.

That single shot from the Appin hillside around 4.30pm on 14 May, 1752, shook the government. It set in motion a chain of dramatic events and presented a murder/mystery/whodunnit with more twists than an Agatha Christie thriller.

In government circles in London there was alarm and anger. How dare these Highland 'savages' murder a government agent going about his lawful government business! But could it mean the first shot of another rebellion? Prince Charles Edward Stewart and his Highland clans had stormed out of their mountains only seven years previously and almost won the crown. The event remained vivid in their minds. That bold adventure had come to a grim conclusion on the battlefield of Culloden on Drumossie Moor.

The government decided to move fast and hard. The word went out: bring the cowardly perpetrators to justice. Immediately. Spare no effort. When they were caught there would be a show trial – and then those unruly Highlanders would know British justice!

The Campbells were incensed at the killing of Glenure. This was also a clan matter. Vengeance was in their every thought. They took control of the investigation and in doing so became the private prosecutors in the case. There were two ready-made targets for their retribution.

Firstly, James Stewart, of Acharn farm, the leading Stewart around, half-brother of the exiled Ardshiel, the Appin Stewarts' chieftain.

James's senior position alone singled him out for special attention. He was arrested the day following the murder as an accomplice. There was not a shred of evidence to link him with the shooting.

Secondly, and prime suspect, was Allan Breck Stewart, professional soldier, well-known Jacobite, a deserter from the British army to the Prince's cause after the Battle of Prestonpans. He took to the heather after the shooting and vanished. He had been heard to issue threats against Glenure in Appin dram shops and was seen on the day in the area of the murder. There was no hard evidence against him other than circumstantial.

That single shot mounted one of the most intense manhunts in Scottish history. Get Allan Breck! That was the command from Appin, Edinburgh and London. Hunt him down. Bring him to justice.

James Stewart was shamefully treated. Held without proper legal representation until the day before his show trial, his home was searched without warrant, and documents which might have helped his case went missing. Evidence was twisted, witnesses' statements were extorted under threat, at least one was held prisoner to prevent his giving evidence.

From the moment that shot rang out in the Wood of Lettermore James's chances of escaping the hangman were bleak. His trial was held in Inveraray, the seat of the Clan Campbell. The jury had 11 members out of 15 all bearing the name Campbell. Some of the jurors were appointed on the recommendations of the murdered man's brother. The Duke of Argyll, the chief of Clan Campbell, presided as Lord Justice-General for Scotland.

In such circumstances, there was only one likely verdict and James was sentenced to hang. Even today some historians consider his execution was a judicial murder. In recent times, a distinguished High Court judge labelled the whole episode "the blackest mark on Scottish legal history".

Allan Breck was never caught. He consistently declared he played no part in the murder, even to his close friends. Years later when he was safe in France and could have been expected to reveal the truth, he continued to maintain that his was not the hand that fired the shot.

James was hanged high. A 30-ft scaffold was erected on the little knoll called Cnap a' Chaolais, at the southern end of where the Ballachulish Bridge is today. His body swung there for almost four

FIGURE 3. Murder scene ... Ian Nimmo takes on the guise of the stricken
Glenure at the exact location of his assassination. Glenure is being tended by his
nephew Mungo, in the form of an Argyll and Sutherland Highlander soldier.
    This reconstruction photograph was taken in 1960 before the Forestry
Commission planted the area. The terrain would have been similar at the time
of the murder. The figures at the top of the hill are also Argyll and Sutherland
Highlanders taking part in a training exercise examining the Appin Murder.
They give an indication of Mungo Campbell's view of the man in the 'short
dark coat' carrying a gun.

years, a highly visible obscenity on a main Highland thoroughfare. Mothers hurried their children past the scene, others looked away across the loch as soon as the horror came into view. A section of 16 soldiers, an officer and a sergeant guarded the remains night and day for almost two years.

The government's message in James's swaying, rotting corpse was stark: Beware! This is what happens to those who stand against us. The days of the Highland clans are over.

Eventually, wind and rain did their work and what was left of James blew down. There was an immediate investigation. How dare the bones be removed without government authority! When it was found the weather was to blame and not recalcitrant Stewarts, the order was given that the bones must be rewired, hoisted back up the scaffold and rehanged. It was deemed that the Stewarts – and Jacobites in general – must continue to be reminded of the folly of rebellion.

At last, one by one the bones began to fall. One night they were carefully gathered, some say by Donald Stewart of Ballachulish, taken to a secret place and the scaffold flung into Loch Linnhe. A plaque on the wall of old Keil Church indicates that, somewhere near, but not at a precise location, James's remains are buried. No chance could be taken that an unforgiving government would have them dug up and hanged once more.

Today Stewarts and Campbells still tend to fall into line with the clan views expressed 250 years ago. The Campbells claim justice was done: Allan Breck fired the shot and James Stewart was guilty 'art and part'. He was properly arrested, tried and hanged.

The Stewarts remain categoric that James was innocent. As the inscription on the memorial on Cnap a' Chaolais declares, James was 'hanged for a crime of which he was not guilty'.

Like the Massacre of Glencoe, the Appin Murder, as the shooting of Colin Campbell has been called, still stirs the old enmities. Those who believe that ancient clan rivalries are a thing of the past and long forgotten are wrong. The rivalries and suspicions of the old warring clans remain just below the surface today.

So whose was the unknown hand that fired the shot that murdered Glenure and brought James Stewart to the gallows?

Tantalisingly, the name of the real assassin has been handed down, generation after generation, among senior Appin Stewarts to this day.

For two-and-a-half centuries the Stewart secret has remained intact. There is no shortage of suspects, and there has been much speculation over the years, but the name will now never be revealed unless one of the Stewarts decides otherwise. Even then, who would believe it? It remains the last great Scottish mystery.

It was the mystery that caught the imagination of writer Robert Louis Stevenson a century after the shooting. The tragic events, the deaths of both Colin Campbell and James Stewart, innocents caught up in a bigger, deeper game, the secret name, the Appin landscape, a love of the Highlands and a fascination with its story, inspired Stevenson to pick up his pen and weave his fiction into the historical facts of the case. The result was *Kidnapped.*

2

The Making of *Kidnapped*

... if you meditate a work of art, you should first long roll
the subject under the tongue to make sure you like the
flavour, before you brew a volume that shall taste of it from
end to end; or if you propose to enter on the field of
controversy, you should first have thought upon the
question under all conditions, in health as well as sickness,
in sorrow as well as in joy.

Robert Louis Stevenson

The inspiration for a bestseller is not usually accompanied by a flash
of lightning. The idea can sometimes take years to germinate. It is
rolled over in the mind, further elements, locations and sub-plots fall
into place haphazardly and unexpectedly, often over long periods. In
the case of Robert Louis Stevenson, however, we know almost
precisely when the idea for *Kidnapped* took wing.

When Stevenson returned from the United States in 1880, it was his
intention to write a *History of the Highlands*. It was a project, he felt,
that would not only advance his desire to be regarded as a serious
writer, but also give him an opportunity to delve into an area of
Scotland that had always caught his imagination. It would also he
hoped give him more financial independence than having to rely on
his father. It was at this time that he applied for the Professorship of
History and Constitutional Law at Edinburgh University. As it turned
out, he was not even called for interview. He had been up north with
his father, with the *History of the Highlands* still much on his mind,
and the subject was discussed in Strathpeffer with Professor Tulloch.
On the way home, they stopped in Inverness, where Thomas
Stevenson bought his son a copy of the record of a Jacobite trial. It

was exactly the kind of book, he considered, that his son would need
for his history.

The unpretentious little volume that was placed in Stevenson's hand
was entitled *The Trial of James Stewart*. The type on the brown leather
spine was old-fashioned, set in gold on a black vertical oblong. On
opening the marbled cover, Stevenson read the following on the first
right-hand printed page:

> The Trial of James Stewart in Aucharn in Duror of Appin, for the
> Murder of Colin Campbell of Glenure, Esq; Factor for His
> Majesty on the forfeited estate of Ardshiel; Before the Circuit
> Court of Justiciary held in Inveraray on Thursday the 21st, Friday
> the 22nd, Saturday the 23rd, and Monday the 25th of September
> last; by his Grace the Duke of Argyll, Lord Justice-General, and
> the Lords Elchies and Kilkerran, Commissioners of Justiciary.

The word 'trial' was in big type in capital letters and took up one line.
'James Stewart' also took up a line but was in smaller italicised capitals.
Where the letter 's' appeared it was written like an 'f' and along the
foot of the page in small type were the words 'Edinburgh: Printed for
G. Hamilton and J. Balfour, 1753'.

On the facing page was a folded-in map, and on opening it
Stevenson's heart gave a jump. Stevenson loved maps. Since childhood
he had made up detailed imaginary maps of his own, inventing
adventures around them, dreaming up exciting names and sometimes
sketching in parts of the scene. Now here was a map that showed
all these features and, intriguingly, much more. Immediately his
imagination began to flare.

The map showed mountain ranges, glens, burns, a great loch, a ferry,
even woods and lochans. Places were marked, too, exotic Highland-
sounding names like Ballachulish and Corrynakeich, Carnoch,
Auchindarrach and Aucharn. These were all neatly printed in type, but
even more exciting, the map was written over in ink in a neat, easily
read hand. Sometimes the letters had flowery flourishes and Stevenson
noted that in concentrating on the writing the spelling of the name
Appin suffered. Appin was clearly the name of the area, but was it
Appin or Appine, he wondered. The writer used both spellings.

In the top right corner of the map, the writing said: 'A Map of the
Country of Appine and its neighbourhood for the trial of James

Stewart'. At the top left corner, six numbers with writing against them, scratched out by the same hand, went vertically down the page. Against the figure 1 at the top it said: 'The house of James Stewart the pannel or prisoner'. Stevenson glanced down the numbers. 'The place where Glenure was murd' read number 4, but the last word was cut short as the writer ran out of space. Then against number 6: 'The place where Breck Stewart retir'd after the murder', again cramped for space and in danger of running into Loch Leven on the map.

Stevenson was entranced. Who really was poor Colin Campbell of Glenure, the murdered man? What was he like as a person? And James Stewart, the pannel or prisoner? Was he innocent or up to the ears in complicity? Clearly he didn't fire the shot. And Breck Stewart must surely mean Allan Breck? As Stevenson began to flick through the pages, he found himself clothing the characters in personality, the events in colour and sound.

Here was the official record with the whole case set out. The charges, witnesses' statements, even 102 named witnesses for the accused. The prosecution and defence legal speeches were there, the sombre verdict, even James Stewart's dignified rejection of it and his forgiveness for those who had brought false witness against him. Everything! As he read, Stevenson could almost hear their voices speak – and the sound of James's body swinging from the gibbet.

Years later, in a letter to his friend, the essayist and art critic Sir Sidney Colvin, checking the spelling of the name Simon Fraser, the crown prosecutor, Stevenson wrote: 'I suppose you are right about Simon. But it is Symon throughout in that blessed little volume my father bought for me in Inverness in the year of grace '81, I believe – the trial of James Stewart, with the Jacobite pamphlet and the dying speech appended – out of which the whole of Davie has slowly been begotten, and which I felt it a kind of loyalty to follow. I really ought to have it bound in velvet and gold, if I had any gratitude! and the best of the lark is, that the name of David Balfour is not anywhere within the bounds of it: a pretty curious instance of the genesis of a book'. Stevenson's mother told a different version of the genesis of *Kidnapped*, but clearly *The Trial of James Stewart* had made its impact on RLS.

David Balfour, of course, was the name of the young hero of *Kidnapped*. A son of the manse, David's home was deep in the most rural part of the Borders, a background and location that hardly prepared him for the high adventure to come. But like other writers before him, Stevenson used the trick of placing innocence in strange and desperate situations, getting inside the head of the almost child-like narrator and vicariously sharing the frightening experiences with his readers. Stevenson took the Balfour name from his mother's side, a daughter of the manse herself, and perhaps his greatest stalwart.

With *The Trial of James Stewart* in his hands, Stevenson did not rush to his desk and begin scribbling. Situations, images, characters and detail had been whispering to his subconscious for years, the writer in him storing them away, random thoughts that might or might not conspire to place words on a page. Masterpieces never written litter the literary graveyards. In Stevenson's case, as far as *Kidnapped* is concerned, the literary spirits who arrange these things smiled benevolently.

The events that worked for Stevenson and the writing of *Kidnapped* began when he was a child. The Stevenson story is well enough known, and does not require retelling here, but inevitably Alison Cunningham must take some credit, although perhaps not in the way intended. 'Cummy', a Fife fisherman's daughter with a taste for hellfire religion, joined the Stevenson family at Edinburgh's Inverleith Terrace. Stevenson dedicated *A Child's Garden of Verses* to her, and his memories of Cummy (his childhood name for her) were always sweet because to him she was a guardian angel. Stevenson's mother had poor health and Cummy took care of everything, from the little boy's coughing fits in the night to telling him bedtime stories.

It was Cummy's stories that sent the boy Stevenson's imagination over the moon. Overdosed with religious fervour, they were told with passion, conviction and a deal of play-acting. Three times Cummy read the bible all the way through to him; her pleasure in telling its stories, shouting out the purple parts where the Deil's evil ways were foiled, had him round-eyed. The vivid bible stories, the battles between good and evil, the pictures accompanying some of the books, sometimes gave him nights when he woke in terror or was afraid to sleep in case he woke up in hell. Cummy once said that Stevenson was 'like other bairns, sometimes naughty', but particularly so when, in her view, he did not give full attention to his prayers and

FIGURE 4. The Stevenson family. The photograph was taken around 1865 and shows the young Robert Louis Stevenson with his parents Thomas and Margaret. Alison Cunningham, Stevenson's nurse, is on his left and the two young women are servants. *The Writers' Museum, Edinburgh.*

hymns. Sometimes, he privately committed little sins just to see if punishment would follow.

With relish Cummy read Hyslop's *The Cameronian Dream,* and the verses of the Rev Robert McCheyne, but there were times when her stories of ghostly visitors, warlocks, kelpies and bogles with horns woke him screaming. Such nightmares may have been partly due to the fevers and ill health that accompanied Stevenson's childhood, for he was always a painfully thin, sickly little boy, coughing with 'chestiness'. On those occasions, when bad dreams and nightmares had him shouting out in dread, his father would come, reassuringly lift him up and comfort him, and tell him other stories, full of different kinds of adventures, until sleep took over again. It was the stories, the words, the rhythms, the cadences of Cummy's spoken words that had as much impact on the child Stevenson as the stories themselves. Apart from dedicating herself to looking after the little boy, it was Cummy who stoked an already fertile imagination and helped him fall in love with words.

On his sixth birthday an aunt gave Stevenson a toy theatre, and this also set his imagination fluttering. The plays and characters from Skelt's Juvenile Drama, with its cut-out figures (penny plain ones, which you could paint yourself, or twopence coloured), gave him hours of fun and make believe. Much of the time he played imaginatively on his own, and here his flights of fancy had free rein. Flashing swords, jolly rogers, tall ships with billowing sails, far-away jungles, intrepid explorers, mountains, redcoat soldiers, pirates, tartans, dirks and bagpipes were in his games. And he was the hero in all the adventures.

Cummy's tales of the Covenanters had also given Stevenson an early interest in Scottish history. As he grew older, he discovered equally absorbing grown-ups' stories in his father's library. *Waverley* and *Rob Roy*, with their Highland settings, particularly caught his interest and already the Highland mountains were beginning to call. It was in *Rob Roy* that Stevenson first encountered Allan Breck and James Stewart.

His father, of course, was a senior member of the Stevenson family of marine engineers, perhaps the greatest in the world at that time. Their legacy was some of the finest lighthouses anywhere – and some were the most difficult to build, situated in hostile territory on remote rocks lashed sometimes by gales and mountainous seas. It was anticipated that the young Robert Louis Stevenson would enter the family business and, in 1867, the year the family acquired their summer retreat of Swanston Cottage, at the foot of the Pentland Hills, Stevenson went to Edinburgh University to study engineering.

From the beginning, Stevenson's heart was not in it. Although he may have been fumbling to identify his life's work, he knew it was not going to be as an engineer. He was dodging lectures at university, tramping the streets of Edinburgh as well as the Pentlands, tasting life, enjoying new experiences, new friends and new freedoms. He was also describing his new life to himself, choosing his words, trying out different words, scribbling them down, filling notebooks. That is how he was. Apart from his studies, life had never been so exciting. He was making fresh assessments of everything, recognising himself, and coming to the conclusion that his background, his love of words, his

sense of adventure and feel for history, his passions and soaring imagination, and his sensitivity to people and places, were the qualities that
might – just might – turn him into a writer. Writing was what he
enjoyed most. Immediately these thoughts began to clarify, his
enthusiasm as always bounded, and he threw himself into the idea.

The element of the engineering apprenticeship he enjoyed most was
site visits. They took him to far-flung corners of Scotland and
were little adventures on their own account. One of these trips was
to the barren islet of Erraid, a dot on the map off the most westerly
point of the Ross of Mull. At the time, in 1870, Dubh Heartach
lighthouse was being erected on a reef 12 miles straight into
the Atlantic, and Erraid was the shore station. The project was
under the direction of his father and his uncle David Stevenson.
On Erraid the granite blocks were measured, sliced and transported
by boat to the solitary Dubh Heartach rocks. The windswept Erraid
was the work base. It had been turned into a bustle of activity:
screeching drills, the hammering of chisels, the howl as the hard
granite resisted, and the shouts of men as the heavy blocks were
manipulated into position.

Erraid made a deep and lasting impression on the 20-year-old
Stevenson. Engineering received hardly a thought. For three
fascinating weeks he explored every corner of the island and crossed
onto the mainland of Mull. After soft Edinburgh, even with its
snapping east wind, the harsh, desolate Mull landscape was like
landing on another planet. The landscapes and seascapes, the skies, the
extraordinary panorama of outcropping rock all the way to Ben More
in the distance, the rain and shrouding mist, the unbelievable sunsets,
gave Stevenson pause. Then would come another sudden weather
change to a shrieking Force 11, as it tore across the island from mid-
Atlantic. The immensity of it all, the vulnerability of those who
ventured in such a wilderness, but also the peace and serenity, were
awesome to the impressionable Stevenson. Erraid made young
Stevenson stop and contemplate.

Here was a different kind of theatre, thought Stevenson, of
mountains, lochs, heaving seas and panoramic backdrops, with
different types of tiny players stepping on its vast stage. Erraid
demanded a different approach, different values. He scribbled in his
exercise books, recorded impressions, descriptions, and composed

some poems, storing details of its tides, rock formations, bays and 'the ferny coverts where the adders hatch, the hollow where the northern sea upfills, the seagull wheeling by with strange sad calls ...', as he put it in an Erraid sonnet. Again they were subconsciously for some future use. How, where and when was still unknown, but a further important location for *Kidnapped* had been put in place.

FIGURE 5. RLS, writer. Stevenson as a young man on the brink of success. The picture was probably taken in Davos around 1881–82. *The Writers' Museum, Edinburgh.*

Back in Edinburgh, after four years of pretending at university, Stevenson had to tell his father that becoming a marine engineer was not going to work. Thomas Stevenson took it well, making allowances for his son as he almost always did. There would have been disappointment, but also understanding that his angular, somewhat eccentric offspring, as he saw it, would probably have been a misfit in the business. Stevenson made it clear he now saw his future as a writer. But the commercial success of having stories published and paid for had still to materialise. Sensible as ever, Thomas advised that his son should at least have a safety net just in case writing success proved elusive. At the back of his mind was the concern that the young Stevenson was wasting his life. His father suggested that the failed engineer should turn his attention to law, which was both responsible and respectable and reassuringly guaranteed a living. Stevenson saw the sense in this and in the autumn of 1871 he entered the Edinburgh firm of W. F. Skene and Peacock for legal training. Four years later he was called to the Scottish bar.

Although Stevenson never practised as an advocate, it was his legal training that gave him a perspective on the trial of James Stewart. The shameful treatment of James played on his mind. From the moment of his arrest, the authorities' denial of access to legal representation or even his family, the revenge of a clan and the vindictiveness of the government, outraged Stevenson's sense of justice. Stevenson was a natural supporter of the underdog, and the more he studied the facts in the Appin case, the more he was drawn to it. The hanging of James, Stevenson considered, had as much to do with justice as stepping on a beetle, yet the court's sentence was carried out in the name of justice. Scotland's most senior lawmen were both prosecutor and judge. In the introduction to *Kidnapped* Stevenson makes it clear he believed Allan Breck was also innocent.

In Stevenson's day, the same bitter clan emotions and the same barbed verbal arrows about the case continued to fly. The hanging of James Stewart was still seen as a miscarriage of justice by one side, and good riddance to a dirty Jacobite by the other. The mystery of who fired the shot still exercised clan and legal debate, historians and ordinary people joined in, articles and letters flowed – and Stevenson looked at his map of the murder site in his volume of *The Trial of James Stewart* and found it all irresistible.

The idea of writing *Kidnapped* had now taken firm hold and had replaced a *History of the Highlands*. In 1881 he wrote from the fashionable Swiss resort of Davos to his friend, poet and critic Sir Edmund Gosse, about his intention to weave a story around the Appin Murder and promised an article about it for *Century Magazine*. In 1882 he set off with his father for Lochearnhead and visited Appin to research *Kidnapped* and study the area and the places named in the trial. He corresponded with John Cameron of Tigh-phuirt, in Glencoe, who gave him information about the Ardshiel family and the MacColls from the Appin area.

From the start, Stevenson set out to write a novel that was not only topographically accurate but also gave a rare historical insight into the condition of the Highlands six years after Culloden. Such is the attention to detail in these respects that the reader frequently falls into the trap of forgetting it is fiction. Although his fiction takes precedence over fact only when Stevenson feels it must for the sake of his story, such is the accuracy of the history, particularly in details of the murder, that the fiction unquestionably bears the ring of authenticity. This is achieved in part by routing *Kidnapped*, as far as Stevenson could, through areas well known to him, and which he could describe with first-hand knowledge. He studied old maps of the period, spoke to people he met on the way to pick up bits of local colour, then his powers of observation, description and imagination took over to weld the fiction and fact together so that they become indistinguishable.

For example, at the beginning of the book, David Balfour leaves the hamlet of Essendean, situated somewhere in Ettrick south of Selkirk, an area well known to the author. You will not find Essendean on any map, but you will find Essenside and Essen Loch set deep in farming country beside the burn of Essen Water that flows down to the village of Ashkirk. Stevenson would have intended the ancient church at Ashkirk to be the centre of the parish of Mr Campbell, David's country minister friend. David could have played a round of golf there today on his old patch. He might have headed for Edinburgh up one of the three main drove roads that ran by Traquair or St Mary's Loch in those days, linking at Peebles, and from there by Romanno Bridge, through Cauldstaneslap in the Pentlands towards Midcalder. Once he arrived at this ancient tryst, or more likely before it, David could have

veered northwards for Edinburgh to bring him out at the west of the
city near Barnton. Perhaps a more direct route would have been the
old stage road, but in any event there was a spider's web of drove
tracks David could have taken – and Stevenson would have known
about them – that could have brought him to Barnton.

Here was the dark, sinister and partly ruined House of Shaws, so
finely drawn that there are still arguments over which house Stevenson
used as the model. Was it Cammo House, which the City of
Edinburgh Council claim was Shaws? Or was it nearby Cramond
Tower? Or perhaps Barnton House, which had a tower, but was
demolished at the end of the First World War? There is nowadays a
'Shaws' in Barnton Avenue, said to be built from the stone of Barnton
House. It carries a triangular stone bearing the initials 'DB'. And so
Stevenson sets the hares running! Or did he simply invent the House
of Shaws? Or steal a bit from each? He knew all these areas so well
and describes them so vividly that David and his route are
entirely believable.

Likewise with the seventeenth-century Hawes Inn, at South
Queensferry, where David Balfour was kidnapped. Stevenson used to
walk over there from Edinburgh, have a meal and a drink, and
sometimes, if he had too much of the latter, he would stay the night.
He canoed on the River Forth with his friend Walter Simpson, son of
Professor Sir James Y. Simpson, of chloroform fame, and both lads
retired to the Hawes Inn afterwards. He knew the scene so well that
it is little wonder that the Hawes Inn, the sailing ships, the sailors with
their tarry pigtails, the smell of the sea, and the brown seaweed
bladders cracking between his fingers, as he put it in *Kidnapped*, are
described so evocatively. We share David's wonder as a first-time
observer of the sea, just as we are part of his innocence when thrust
into high and dangerous adventures.

Kidnapped was begun early in 1885 in the house he named
Skerryvore in Bournemouth. It was initially written, he said,
'partly as a lark, partly as a pot boiler' for *Young Folk*. But soon the
characters began to take over and he realised he had something
here that was important. 'I think David is on his feet, and (to my
mind) a far better story and far sounder at heart than *Treasure Island*.
I have no earthly news, living entirely in my story, and only
coming out of it to play patience,' he wrote to his father. In fact,

FIGURE 6. *Kidnapped* first appeared as a serial in *Young Folks Paper* on May 1, 1886, published by James Henderson, of Fleet Street, London, priced one penny. Later that year the story was reprinted in book form by Cassell, London, and Scribner's of New York. Film, stage and radio versions have travelled the world ever since.

what was emerging through the pages of *Kidnapped* was a writer coming of age. *Kidnapped* confirmed Stevenson as an accomplished novelist with an ability to grip the imagination and create convincing characters of depth and complexity, delivered in a simple, direct style with pace.

He was a fast writer. *Kidnapped* took about five months to produce, although ill health intervened, inspiration flagged, he lost intensity, and he even gave up for a time. By January, 1886, exhaustion slowed the words and ideas in the last chapters. He was 'almost worked out', as he commented, but by spring that year the book was finished. He was concerned about the Highland part. For an area of Scotland so close to his heart he wanted it just right. Had there been time, he would probably have preferred to return to the Highlands for more detail, particularly to the Ben Alder, Rannoch, Glenlyon and Glen Dochart stretches. 'I don't think it will be so interesting to read, but it is curious and picturesque,' he said. He was irritated when his editor told him to write *Kidnapped* without 'much broad Scotch in it, as a little of that goes a long way with our readers'.

Stevenson's original idea was to include the Appin Murder, the trial of James Stewart and James's hanging all in *Kidnapped*. At that stage, the working title was *David Balfour*, but covering so much ground was proving too ambitious, his health was giving way, the book was becoming unwieldy and he did not have the energy to solve the problem. At last he took the advice of his friend Sidney Colvin. Colvin suggested that the events of 1752 be turned into two books – *Kidnapped* to be drawn to a close with David Balfour coming into his inheritance on his return to Edinburgh. The sequel would meet again with the same central characters, but include the trial of James, his grim death and Allan Breck's escape to the Continent. Whether a love interest for David was developed at that time is uncertain, but *Catriona*, the shy, Highland beauty, daughter of Rob Roy MacGregor's disreputable son James More, gave her name to the title.

The year 1886 was a high point for Stevenson. In January *The Strange Case of Dr Jekyll and Mr Hyde* was published by Longmans Green in London and Charles Scribner's in New York; and in July *Kidnapped, being Memoirs of the Adventures of David Balfour in the year 1751* was published in book form to acclaim by Cassell in London and

FIGURE 7. 'They broke before him like water ... the sword in his hands flashed like quicksilver in the huddle of our fleeing enemies; and at every flash there came the scream of a man hurt.' Allan Breck puts the crew of the brig *Covenant* to flight at the siege of the round-house off Mull. An illustration from *Young Folks Paper* of May 22, 1886. *The Writers' Museum, Edinburgh*

Scribner's. It was 1893, two years before Stevenson's death, when *Catriona* was finally published in the United Kingdom.

In the planning of *Kidnapped*, one of Stevenson's main problems was how to find a device to transport David Balfour from Edinburgh to within striking distance of the murder scene in Appin. The answer came in a flash. Have him kidnapped! It would serve as the means as well as the title. So scheming Uncle Ebenezer has David sweet-talked aboard the brig *Covenant*, then lying at anchor at South Queensferry, bound for the Carolinas. David is dunted on the head on the instruction of Captain Hoseason, and thrown below decks. When at last he emerges, he is well at sea. David is given the job of cabin boy as the *Covenant* heads around the north of Scotland, buffeted by storms. To find less hostile waters, Hoseason turns the *Covenant* southwards. They run down a small boat in thick mist and only one man survives. With great agility he hurls himself upwards and manages to climb aboard the brig. His fine clothes tell he is a man of status, a

FIGURE 8. The Hawes Inn at South Queensferry was given mention by both
Stevenson and Sir Walter Scott. It dates back to a seventeenth-century private
house, although there has been an inn around the ferry point since early days.
The deal to kidnap David Balfour was sealed between his uncle and Captain
Hoseason, of the brig *Covenant*, in the Hawes Inn. Stevenson canoed and swam
in the sea here and sometimes spent the night in the Hawes.

sword is at his side, a cocked hat on his head and his eyes hold a kind
of dancing wildness. Here is a man, thinks David, he would rather call
his friend than his enemy. It is the first meeting of the Jacobite Allan
Breck Stewart and David Balfour.

Allan Breck is carrying a belt of gold, money gathered in Appin
from Stewart tenants to keep their leader, Ardshiel, in decent exile in
France. The ship's murderous crew want their fingers on it, but David
stands four-square with Allan and the two successfully fight them off.

Miraculously, David and Allan remain uninjured, but they have killed and wounded some of the sailors. A wind picks up and the under-manned *Covenant* gathers speed as she runs before it into dangerous waters off Mull. Stevenson moves the Torran Rocks a few miles northwards and the brig strikes and founders. A wave carries David overboard. Down he gurgles, hitting out like a drowning man, then desperately manages to clutch a piece of flotsam and cling to it. He tumbles, splutters, flails, until he is flung into quieter water in the lee of a dark shore. David takes up the tale:

> In about an hour of kicking and splashing, I had got well in
> between the points of a sandy bay surrounded by low hills. The
> sea was here quite quiet; there was no sound of any surf; the
> moon shone clear; and I thought in my heart that I had never
> seen a place so desert and desolate.

And that is how Robert Louis Stevenson managed to land his young hero, David Balfour, more dead than alive, on the strange little island of Erraid …

3

The Islet

How David Balfour was shipwrecked on the tiny isle of Erraid, and 250 years later I discover his landing place, learn of a dog in space, find a deserted street in the middle of nowhere, hear the call of an island, and find myself cut off by the tide.

The island of Erraid is a jumble of granite rocks with heather, rough grass and bracken between. It is guarded on the seaward side by a menacing array of contorted rock shapes – miniature fortresses, sinister submarines and stone sea monsters. The only safe landing place on its wild Atlantic-facing shoreline is a small but beautiful sandy bay. The water here is as bright blue-green as a Samoan beach scene. The likeness stops abruptly there. Instead of palms trees, wizened, stunted oaks, hazels, birches and bushes, dwarfed by salted winds, cling to the shallow soil. Even the granite rocks look sculpted by aeons of wind and rain. In the centre of the island are a valley and a small hill. From the hilltop there is a panorama that will hold you spellbound. View it in silence. If you can, go there alone.

It is the view that gripped Robert Louis Stevenson. Stevenson's first sight of Erraid was 'framed in the round bullseye of a cabin port' when he was 15 years of age and on a cruise with his parents. David Balfour's arrival on Erraid was unscheduled. He clung for dear life to the wrecked *Covenant*'s spare yard, more drowned than alive, the roaring of the breakers and sea-chill numbing his senses. He staggered ashore in the dead of night with the moon high, on that very sandy bay facing the open sea. How do we know? Well, the Ordnance Survey map has it named as Balfour's Bay. Clearly, a *Kidnapped* reader or Stevenson supporter in the past has taken the trouble to officially christen Erraid's blue lagoon with David's name as if it had been fact.

The first time I saw Erraid, the sea was exploding off the rocks like thunder. I had come up from Oban on the old *George V*, with a 40-pound rucksack and my former army camouflage jacket on my back. It was 1960 and I was about to yomp, as they say today, from Erraid back to Edinburgh in the footsteps of David Balfour and Allan Breck. I wasn't sure what to expect. I had the notion of examining the *Kidnapped* trail in two timewarps: as it was in 1752, when the action took place, and as it was in 1960. As it has turned out, I am now looking at it in three timewarps because at the beginning of the twenty-first century, the changes in Scotland and along the route have been almost as profound.

The *George V* dropped me and a handful of others off Iona. We had difficulty in clambering down its heaving side into a dinghy that landed us on Columba's sacred isle. It was raining and the wind was rising. There was no big, powerful, car-carrying ferry in 1960. I had to call twice to Fionnphort from the Iona telephone box to see if ferryman Angus McKechnie could lift us over to Mull's mainland. Angus was reluctant. The sea was running too high, he said. He would be over as soon as he could. Eventually, we spotted Angus's little white boat making its way towards us. It was a now-you-see-him-now-you-don't crossing as the white horses pranced. At one point he seemed to vanish. I remember thinking: do I really want to cross in this?

I remember, too, one of the three other passengers reading a copy of the *Daily Express*, which was a broadsheet then. He's taking a long time to read the front page, the journalist in me thought. He was attempting to shelter the paper while the wind tried to whip it into the sea. Must be something important, I guessed. Then I saw the headline. The Russians had sent a dog into space. I glanced up at the grey clouds scudding angrily across the sky and tried to peer beyond. I turned to Angus. 'You can hardly believe it,' I shouted against the wind. 'There's a dog somewhere up there in a spacecraft whirling its way round the earth. Fantastic!'

I have never forgotten his response. It was laconic, polite, but perhaps with just a hint of indulgence. 'Aye', he shouted back. 'It's wonderful what they can do these days.' That's all. But his eyes never left the water. He was plotting our course, examining each wave individually, assessing the danger, eyeing the Mull shore, minimising risk. Our lives were in his hands. That short journey in Angus

McKechnie's wee seacraft propelled by an inboard motor across the
Sound of Iona with the white horses leaping all around, put the whole
space programme for me into perspective.

After that his conversation amounted to four further words. He
pointed to a long, low, dark and rocky shape in the water west and
beyond Fionnphort. 'Erraid!' he roared, with his hands cupped. 'David
Balfour's island.'

Angus probably never appreciated how sincere were my thanks
when we reached the Mull pier. My own colour, I think, was green,
the other three passengers were varying shades of green, grey and
white. One passenger deposited his breakfast halfway over, thankfully
on the leeward side. I checked my map. That way, I said out loud to
myself. Along that little road from the centre of Fionnphort village.
I heaved up my rucksack and set off briskly down the track
towards Erraid.

The tide was out and that was good news. My first task was to test
David Balfour's experience that Erraid was tidal. Three full days David
spent on Erraid after the shipwreck, unable to cross to the Ross of
Mull, because he found himself cut off by sea on all sides. After his
first quick reconnoitre, David believed cruel fate had cast him on an
island where he was likely to freeze or starve to death. Limpets and
winkles, or buckies, as David called them, were his only diet; the rain
poured incessantly, his teeth chattered and the raw shellfish made him
ill. Erraid was the most unhappy period of his whole adventures.
When two Mull fishermen appeared in a cobble and laughed at his
plight, poor David was almost beside himself with anger and self-pity.
They laughed at him, of course, because at low tide it was possible to
splash across the narrows on the south-east corner of the island.

Looking back on my own first visit to Erraid, I realise now how
gloriously unprepared I was for my march back to Edinburgh along
the *Kidnapped* Trail. I had little knowledge in those days of Mull, or
of the Appin Murder for that matter, and therefore much of what I
encountered was new to me. It was *Kidnapped*, the Appin mystery and
the wild terrain that had caught my fancy. I realised, of course, it was
no small undertaking to cross Scotland on foot through some tough,
mountainous and lonely country, but I was as fit as a stag and
considered I was well able to look after myself. After all, I was a
reasonably experienced climber and only three years previously I had

FIGURE 9. David Balfour's island. Erraid today from the mainland of the Ross of Mull. The buildings and pier in the centre of the picture were erected by the Stevensons as the shore station for the construction of Dubh Heartach Lighthouse. It then became home to the lighthouse keepers and their families. The interiors of the houses have now been refurbished and they are in use again as a base of the Findhorn Community, the islet's custodians. *Alun John*

been an officer in the old Royal Scots Fusiliers. I had a taste for history, a passion for Robert Louis Stevenson and his writings, and, in my view, it was a simple case of have maps will march, with my much-thumbed Stevenson classic tucked safely in my rucksack. David Balfour's adventures gave me a sense of adventuring into what was unknown territory for me, too.

I had two surprises on the short walk from Fionnphort. The first came as I drew closer to Erraid. Was that really a row of cottages I saw on the island facing the mainland? There was even a pier below. Strange, there was no sign of life. I had envisaged a barren, uninhabited island with only seabirds for company. It was still too far to see the buildings in detail, but they were obviously substantially stone-built and there was a large walled garden in front of them. About 600 yards away, towards a corner of the island close to the mainland, was a white cottage with a red roof. As I watched, a figure appeared for a few moments, then vanished round the side of the house. I walked on thinking this was an unexpected turn of events. People on Erraid!

My second surprise was to be suddenly confronted by an ancient house straight out of a *Kidnapped* filmset. It was tiny, very low and built of boulders stuck together with mortar. The thatched roof was misshapen, held in place by fishermen's nets sewn together by rope. Large dangling rocks hung from the nets or further ropes to keep the roof in place. The chimney had blown over to a rakish angle and was smoking. A single, tiny window was at the front, and the door was propped open by two wooden boxes. It wasn't quite a traditional blackhouse, but certainly a close cousin and in the style, I learned later, of that corner of Mull.

I stared in disbelief. It must be a fisherman's bothy, I guessed. Probably used as a store, or shelter, a place to rest and brew a mug of tea when the weather turned nasty. As I looked, a figure stepped through the doorway. It was an elderly woman and she, too, was straight out of *Kidnapped*. She could have been the wife of the old gentleman who befriended David as he escaped from the island, fed him cold grouse and gave him a bed for the night. The old lady I met wore a black woolly hat pulled down over her ears, a black woolly jumper, a long black skirt, black woolly stockings and a pair of very stout black shoes. She did not smile.

"Hello," I said. "Can you tell me the easiest place to cross onto Erraid?"

There was a long pause. Then she addressed me in Gaelic. Occasionally, she gestured in the direction I was going. I tried to join in the conversation to explain I hardly had a word of the language. Occasionally, I picked up 'erish', repeated several times, which is the Gaelic pronunciation of Erraid.

Later I learned that this was old Mary Cameron, a worthy of the area, and this had been her home for many years. Her eyesight was failing, but she still managed to walk the two miles into Fionnphort for her shopping and then back again. Mary offered me a mug of tea, but I gave her a polite wave and moved on. Our discussion in Gaelic was going nowhere, and unless I stepped on to Erraid before the tide turned, so was I.

FIGURE 10. In 1960 this was the home of Mary Cameron, who lived alone opposite Erraid. Mary was one of the worthies of the area and her traditional home was typical of a form of 'blackhouse' common to this corner of Mull. Mary and her house have now long gone.

As I turned away, she said in lilting Highland English and with a smile: 'I think you will enjoy Erraid. It is a lovely place'.

As I walked along the rocky beach, I put to flight a small flock of greylag geese, which alighted with complaining honks 200 yards ahead. In most other places, I thought, these wary birds would be up and over the horizon. I was disturbing hares, curlews, oystercatchers, sandpipers, two herons, numerous gulls, including arctic terns, a variety of ducks and flocks of small birds too distant to identify as they fed from the tidal flats. The geese rose again as I approached, only to settle in front of me for a second time, then take the air as I drew close, but then sensibly land behind me to carry on feeding as before. A buzzard gave me a glare from a rock and I thought, wonderful, Mull is the nearest thing to being a nature reserve.

My steps took me to a corner of what looked like the narrowest point between Erraid and the mainland. This is the moment of truth, I remember thinking. Will I be able to wade over like David Balfour or will my pack drop me like a stone to the bottom of 20 feet of salt water? Was Robert Louis Stevenson accurate, or had he simply made it all up?

FIGURES II AND I2.   The tide is out ... and that meant David Balfour
could escape from his Erraid 'prison' by splashing across the narrow channel
separating the islet from the Mull mainland. After the shipwreck, David spent
three of the most unhappy days of his journey on Erraid, cut off as he thought
by sea on all sides. The picture below shows Erraid becoming an island again as
the tide turns. Stevenson's accuracy on such points of geographic detail, woven
into the historical facts, gives authenticity to the whole of David Balfour's
wanderings. *Alun John*

The narrowest point turned out to be a sandy channel of about 400 yards. There were bright little sea pools here and there, but I could see from the tide mark on the low cliffs that the channel had held up to 15 feet of water only hours previously. Stevenson was right! At low tide, it was possible to splash over almost dryshod, but when the tide turned Erraid quickly became an island again.

This experience gave me a tremendous boost. A country lad like David Balfour, a satellite island never crossed my mind until I read *Kidnapped*. Had the description of Erraid turned out to be a piece of Stevenson invention, I think I would have explored the islet, walked across Mull, climbed Ben More, then caught the boat back to Oban and home. But somehow I was thrilled with the knowledge that the Erraid crossing was just as David Balfour described it. The journey ahead had come alive. The rain stopped, there was a glint of watery sunshine that sent the mica in the granite rocks gleaming. I took the last few strides at a run and fairly jumped on to David Balfour's island.

I decided to head for the highest point to take my bearings. The walking was rough and strenuous, granite slabs have to be navigated or clambered over, bracken and heather clumps have hidden rocks and potholes and I walked warily. But Erraid also holds pleasant little meadows and quiet hollows, heathery bowers, wild flowers, sudden valleys in miniature – and granite rock everywhere. Rocks and rocks and rocks. As far as the eye can see. Rocks that crystallised from a molten mass on this corner of the Ross of Mull more than 400 million years ago.

I did not take the top of the hill at a charge because, as I climbed higher, the views from Erraid began to unfold. The clouds were lifting and I halted every few strides just to drink in the Erraid experience. To describe such a panorama is unsatisfactory because it instantly becomes personal, something felt. The moment belongs to the beholder and is lost in trying to communicate it meaningfully to others. Enough to say that the Erraid landscape is primaeval, harsh and beautiful. It stretches into the distance on all sides. It combines seascape and mountains. When Columba arrived from Ireland 1,400 years ago, bringing the Christian word with him, he could just as easily have chosen Erraid for his church as Iona, a couple of miles away. It would be surprising if Columba or his monks had not visited Erraid, for both islands share the same sense of eternity. It would also be surprising if those Viking raiders, the scourge of Columba and Iona, did not anchor their longboats in Balfour's Bay.

I found a suitably comfortable rock, took off my rucksack, sat down and looked and looked.

Stevenson has been criticised for failing to describe Erraid in more detail. Of course, he was then an accomplished writer earning a living by his pen, and *Kidnapped* is essentially a novel of pace and adventure. It was written 16 years after his stay on Erraid, yet the description of the terrain and David's sufferings, often achieved broadly by hints and allusions rather than fine detail, remains accurate and vivid. But taking into account his other writings about the island, it may be that the harshness rather than Erraid's peace and beauty made the most impact on the young Stevenson.

I have come to know Erraid well over the years. I find it a special place. The downside is that every time I visit Mull I feel I must also visit Erraid. It is inexplicable. Erraid is no more than a rock-strewn nothing speck, but I have felt drawn to it ever since that first visit. These feelings are unrelated to Stevenson or David Balfour, and the odd thing is that everyone I know who also knows the island really well – a handful of people – feels the same way. If you're switched on to the right wavelength, Erraid somehow calls.

There was no sign of life from the houses I saw from the opposite shore. I observed them from above. They formed a single street in the middle of nowhere. They were in excellent condition, made of thick granite blocks, placed one on top of the other and obviously built by craftsmen. I remember thinking, these walls will still be standing a thousand years hence. The large gardens behind their thick granite dyke were overgrown. The street was silent. I went down and knocked at a door. Not a sound.

There was the same response at several other doors. It was almost eerie. A remote island, a street of five double houses, all in excellent order, but not a person in sight. No sound of radio, no smell of cooking, no washing on the line. How strange! I walked down to the pier where there were other buildings. No boat. I went back up to the street and tried a doorhandle. The door was unlocked. I stepped inside and the room was scrubbed clean. I tried several of the houses. All were unlocked. Such trust, I thought. One room held pieces of furniture neatly stacked. There was also a child's wooden toy. How

mysterious! A whole community seemed to have lived here. Who were
they? Surely they must all have decided to leave together. But why?
Or did someone make them leave?

But of course, the lighthouse keepers! These must be the homes of
the people who built Dubh Heartach. These were Stevenson-built
houses. This is where Robert Louis Stevenson must have lived. But
which was his house? And I then remembered that after Dubh
Heartach and Skerryvore lighthouses were completed, Erraid became
the shore station for the keepers and their families. So where were
they now?

I began to stroll down to the white cottage. The sun was up, the
wind had dropped, only Ben More in the distance still had a wisp of
cloud around its bare summit. The figure I had seen previously
appeared again. This time I could see it was another elderly lady. She
hadn't noticed me and I decided immediately not to knock at her door.
A stranger appearing out of the blue at the only inhabited house on a
deserted island could start alarm bells jangling, especially when the
nearest neighbour is a mile away and on another shore. In any event, I
would soon be off the island, heading across Mull, and the lady need
not be bothered or even know of my presence. But I admired her
independence living alone like that at her age at the back of the cut-off
beyond. Good for you, I whispered, and climbed back up the hill, this
time with my map out, to see if I could find Balfour's Bay.

On the way I came across a little circular hut with a pointed roof
on high ground with a clear view out to sea. Then excitedly I
remembered again – surely this was the Stevenson observatory that
housed the powerful telescope during the building of Dubh Heartach.
I remembered reading how those ancient lighthouse creators were able
to focus on that spiteful black rock out in the Atlantic to see if the
weather was quiet enough for work. It could be fearsome out there
and the Stevenson experience was that they could count on only three
months out of 12 for construction.

I came over a rise, and suddenly there was Balfour's Bay below me!
Unmistakable on a shoreline bristling with menacing rocks that extend
into the sea to form a jagged barrier. In this threatening array,
Balfour's Bay is serene and peaceful, blue and golden. But it was a
miracle, I considered, that David was able to pass those rocks
unscathed and arrive in this narrow inlet to stagger safely ashore. Even

as I watched, the rocks were fracturing the waves, sending the spray flying. They made hungry, sucking noises at my feet.

I could picture David dragging himself out of that little bay, tired as he had never been before, as he put it, not daring to sit down in case he froze, then taking off his shoes to walk to and fro upon the sand, beating his breast to restore circulation and bring a little warmth to his shivering limbs. I looked around. No one was in sight. Apart from the lady who lived alone in the white house, Erraid was deserted. A further check over my shoulder. Then I, too, took off my boots and socks – but unlike David Balfour I waded into his bay for an irresistible paddle.

It is one thing to sit safely in a warm home in civilised Edinburgh, poring over maps and plotting routes that would take me back to Edinburgh along the *Kidnapped* Trail; it is entirely another matter to stand on Erraid, as near moonscape as I could envisage, with the long miles stretching ahead and the sky darkening with clouds again.

FIGURE 13. Safety at last ... it was into the quiet, green waters of this Erraid cove, set among jagged rocks on a ferocious coastline, that David Balfour staggered ashore after the *Covenant* was lost. Stevenson was able to describe the island in detail after living on Erraid for three memorable weeks in 1870. The cove is now marked 'Balfour's Bay' on Ordnance Survey maps.

Spectacular country all along the way, yes, but also wild, remote and desolate and some of those miles were vertical. However, my morale had received a fillip with the discovery of the old observatory, Balfour's Bay and the fact that Erraid was, as David described it, indeed an island at high tide.

The tide! I had forgotten the tide. I half ran back over the hill to the channel. But instead of the sandy land bridge, the water was neck-deep and rising. I was too late! By my own folly I had succeeded in doing a David Balfour! I had become so engrossed with exploring the island that I had lost track of time. I couldn't believe it. I also noticed a blurring grey mist was beginning to approach from the sea, already blunting the outlines of the farthest island and rocks. Longingly I gazed at the opposite shore, so close but now out of reach, as the water deepened. The first big plops of rain reminded me I was about to sample a night on Erraid in David Balfour conditions. I made an instant decision: on no account would I eat raw winkles.

4

Heaven and Hell on Erraid

How David Balfour spent four days of misery on Erraid,
Robert Louis Stevenson saw a frenzy of work, I find his
house, meet unusual residents, hear a silkie cackle, have a
close encounter with an otter, and confirm David's island
can be both hell and heaven.

From Erraid dawn breaks behind the great peak of Ben More. Between
island and mountain is a desert wilderness of rock, heather, bog and
Loch Scridain. When the sun rises Ben More is something to behold.
Shades of blue, silver, pink, sometimes red, brush its brow and the
colours alter within minutes. In winter, with a blasting of snow and a
glint of sun, Ben More can transmute into a shining mountain of gold.
But then that well-known leaden wash splashes across the sky, rocks
and sea darken, the raindrops grow fatter, fall faster and louder, and
Ben More becomes the Invisible Man. This is the moody Erraid
Robert Louis Stevenson knew and little has changed today except that
the islet is quieter.

Erraid is now owned by a Dutchman. That is something
neither Stevenson nor David Balfour would have envisaged. He
arrives on the island for four weeks in the year accompanied by
his extended family and friends – around 200 of them – and they
have a jolly time. They take over what were the old lighthouse
keepers' cottages and overflow into hotels and bed-and-
breakfast accommodation in Fionnphort and even some to Iona.
They swim in Balfour's Bay, fish for lobsters, birdwatch, sail, walk
on Mull, play soak-me-if-you-can with the spray as the waves strike
the rocks, gather mussels, and on one of the long-light summer
evenings they throw a party and invite the neighbours from across
the water.

What makes a Dutchman want to buy a remote Scottish island? It was a question I was able to put to the owner, M. van der Sluis. His answer reflects the shrinking world and changing face of Scotland – but who could argue with his motives? 'When I was a child I used to go with my parents to one of the Dutch islands in the north during school holidays', he told me. 'As children we felt totally free, roaming through the dunes, fishing and beachcombing. In the 1970s more and more tourists came and a lot of fences were erected to protect nature. As the years passed, we hoped we could find a place, somewhere, where our children could experience the same kind of freedom and be part of nature.

'During the first visit to Erraid, the weather was wonderful and we immediately fell in love with the island. Our family and friends straddle all ages, even an octogenarian goes with us in the summer. First of all it was the children and now it is the grandchildren doing exactly the same things. We think that is good. We walk the garden walls and fish for shrimps. We like to sit on the big rocks at Balfour's Bay. We visit the seals, always on the same rocks, and we love the smell of bog myrtle and heather. That is why we came to Erraid.'

The custodians of Erraid are members of the Findhorn Community who live in 'Lighthouse Street', as I call it, for the rest of the year. They bring guests to the island from across the world. Apart from Erraid granite, which no-one wants now, peace and tranquillity are the island's most prolific resources. Some visitors come in search of escape or to find a simpler, more natural lifestyle, more satisfying and more meaningful than the racetrack a large section of the world whirls around today. New values are to be discovered on Erraid, they believe, and the Findhorn Community team helps them on their way.

When the island changed ownership and the Community people also moved in there were misgivings among local folk, and also among those who valued Erraid from much farther afield. Their fear was that such a very special place would be spoiled. For their separate reasons, however, both the van der Sluis family and the Findhorn Community also recognise Erraid as special – and are passionate about keeping it that way. Together they have become a positive force in the island's interests. The lighthouse keepers' cottages have been improved, the pier has been re-built, the large walled garden is more productive than it has ever been. Erraid now has electricity

FIGURE 14. 'Lighthouse Street' on Erraid. The cottages stand as a testimony
to the Stevensons as master craftsmen. They were erected over 120 years ago and
remain as comfortable and weather-proof today as they were then. The gardens
on the right behind the wall have never been more productive and the iron
railing is to a Stevenson design. In recent times, the weather-worn railing was
replaced exactly to the Stevenson specification by the present Dutch owner of
the island.

and a telephone. A telephone on Erraid! Even the attractive iron railing
along the top of the garden wall, designed by the Stevensons, but
suffering a century of Erraid weather, has been remade and replaced
the way the Stevensons planned it and precisely to the same
Stevenson design. The cottages have been modernised inside,
but outside they look just as they did when the young RLS arrived
more than 130 years ago.

The Community have now been on Erraid for around 25 years. Paul
Johnston, a Geordie with the accent to prove it, and a member of the
Findhorn Community, gave me an insight into the life they lead on
that tiny pile in the vastness of sea and rocks. We stood in the garden
behind its wall of granite, two-and-a-half feet thick and strong enough
to repel a Viking raid. A flock of goldfinches descended as we spoke,
red crowns bobbing, as they picked at thistles in a corner. 'The wildlife
here is amazing', said Paul, catching on to my interest. 'Eider duck
gather down there below us, all kinds of seabirds, and a friendly seal

is visiting us just now. We see him between the piers as we cross to the mainland.

'Our garden is important to us. Not just because we eat from it throughout the year, but because working the earth is somehow fundamental. We grow many different kinds of vegetables and fruits here. The sandy soil helps it and so does the seaweed. Sometimes, after a storm, we find the wind has spread the seaweed for us.

'Across the year we receive up to 300 guests. They share and play a part in our island life. That could mean digging potatoes in the garden, helping us with the firewood, looking after some of our animals. It gives our visitors a feel and taste of the kind of lives we lead. We get all sorts, architects, doctors, even the manager of an overseas chain store has stayed with us.

'There is a lot of spiritual power in this whole area. We chose Erraid because it's a place of light energy. There are not so many places like this in the world. A lot of contemplation goes on here. We even have our own meditation house for anyone who wants to use it. People get different things from Erraid. Many discover new perspectives. We make sure our guests have plenty of time for themselves. Just looking and listening is important here and keeping the island's integrity is vital.'

At 6pm a hand bell is rung up and down the 'street'. Dinner is served. Doors opened and residents strolled to the cottage designated as the meeting and dining area. I was invited to join them, and around a dozen sat down at two tables. Everything was easy, informal, but heads bowed respectfully for grace and then, with great decorum, in that humble cottage in such spectacular surroundings, we delved in. Excellent! Paul was cook on this occasion and received his just congratulations with modesty.

The conversation turns to my Stevenson interests and also my knowledge of the island over so many years. Yes, I knew Katie McGillivray, who lived in the red-roofed house down by the shore. Used to be a Queen Alexandra's nurse and was in the First World War, you know, a delightful, caring person. Lived alone on the island for years. She was born in that cottage, but came home eventually to nurse her mother. Never wanted to leave again. It was Katie's wish to be buried on Erraid. No, I didn't meet Ella Horsey. I remember she wrote a book about her seven years on Erraid. She left just before I arrived. Oh yes, I knew Christine Gibson well enough. She was with the BBC for years. I used to have a cuppa and a chat with Christine every time I came to the island. Christine found her true home on Erraid and she, too, never wanted to leave that same house where Katie lived. The channel has silted up quite a lot since I first came here, you know. If it goes on like that Erraid will stop being an island in a century or two.

It was all friendly, chatty, normal, enjoyable. The Findhorn people said they would take me back to the mainland in their boat, now with an outboard, rather than the hard row against the wind I once experienced. This time I never gave the tide a thought. Everyone commented on the workmanship that went into the building of those Stevenson houses. In a century-and-a-half, the granite blocks have never moved an inch. The buildings stand as true as the day they were built. It is impossible even to slip a knifeblade between the blocks. New guttering was required in recent times, which caused a problem because modern drills could not cope with the tough granite. Yet in Stevenson's day, the 'primitive' drills could cut holes for blasting three metres deep. The original fireplaces are still in the cottages, but efficient modern wood-burning stoves have been installed. In winter, when the big storms crash, another log goes on the fire, and everyone stays inside in the warm. Sometimes it is almost impossible to stand against the wind, yet winter is arguably the most beautiful of Erraid's seasons, when Ben More slips into its Disney filmset repertoire and occasionally the Northern Lights flicker across the sky.

It was so different when the 20-year-old Robert Louis Stevenson landed in the summer of 1870. Dubh Heartach was still two years from completion and Erraid was a buzz of industry as its shore station. Dubh Heartach was the third of the Stevensons' offshore lighthouses, 15 miles out into the Atlantic on a reef infamous among seamen. Next stop was Labrador 1,600 miles away. The rocks were isolated, took the full brunt of heavy swells and demonic storms, a ships' graveyard for as long as anyone could remember. The sinking of the *Bussorah* on the Dubh Heartach rocks, with 23 hands lost, on its maiden voyage in January, 1863, highlighted the need for a light, and the ferocious winter storms of three years later, which accounted for 24 wrecked or distressed vessels, made it urgent. These extreme conditions presented the Stevensons with another dangerous and difficult engineering challenge.

FIGURE 15. Lighthouse lookout. This was the hut that the Stevensons used as an observatory on Erraid. It housed a powerful telescope to assess sea conditions during the building of Dubh Heartach. Such was the ferocity of the sea on those black rocks that building work was limited to only a few months in the year. The old observatory has now been rebuilt.

Robert Louis Stevenson explains best what life was like on the shore station:

> On Isle Erraid, there was a good quarry of granite, two rows of sheds, two travelling cranes, railways to carry the stones, a stage on which, course after course, the lighthouse was put experimentally together and then taken down again to be sent piece-meal out to the rock, a pier for the lighters, and a lookout place furnished with a powerful telescope by which it could be observed whether the weather was clear [and] how high the sea was running on Dubh Heartach and so judge whether it were worthwhile to steam out on the chance of landing.

> In a word, there was a stirring village of some [fifty] souls, on this island which, four years before, had been tenanted by one fisherman's family and a herd of sheep. The life in this little community was highly characteristic. On Sundays only, the continual clink of tools from quarry and workyard came to an

FIGURE 16. The making of a lighthouse. Dubh Heartach was built layer by
layer on Erraid to ensure that it fitted, then the granite blocks were carefully
packed in straw and shipped out to the storm-lashed rock. The picture shows five
of the top layers being tested on Erraid around 1870. *Northern Lighthouse Board*

end, perfect quiet then reigned throughout the settlement, and
you saw workmen leisurely smoking their pipes about the green
enclosure, and they and their wives wearing their Sunday clothes
(from association of ideas, I fancy), just as if they were going to
take their accustomed seats in the crowded church at home. As
for the services at Erraid, they were held in one of the wooden
bothies, the audience perched above the double tier of box beds
gathered round the table. Mr Brebner read a sermon and the
eloquent prayer which was specially written for the Scottish
Lighthouse Service, and a voluntary band and precentor led the
psalms.

Mr Alan Brebner was the superintendent of work. The young
Stevenson struck up a friendship with a teenage lad who was probably
Alan's son. The two youngsters had the run of Erraid and the writer
within Stevenson noted it all. Those Sunday services in the bothy must
have been moving, with the waves breaking feet away, the wind
hymning, the voices raised in song, man against nature, savage and
awesome, and the fearful thoughts of everyone on 6am the following

morning when the menfolk would be heading out to those angry rocks again, sometimes still in winter darkness. The foreman builder of the project was a Mr Robert Goodwillie, who meticulously kept a journal. It was thanks to him that details of Stevenson were recorded as well as an almost blow-by-blow account of the building of a great lighthouse. Much of this emerged only in the last few years following research by the distinguished Stevenson scholar Roger Swearingen, which led to the publication of a booklet by Stevenson titled *The New Lighthouse on the Dhu Heartach Rock, Argyllshire*. The quote above describing Erraid is taken from this booklet. It was an unpolished essay and the parentheses interestingly indicate missing words or checks on fact still to be made by Stevenson.

One of the encouraging aspects of modern Erraid is that children are once more on the island. Findhorn custodian Paul Johnston's own little boy will go to Bunessan school when he is five. An alert eye will be kept on the weather, winds and tide, until he is home safely. It has always been thus with island folk.

At one time 24 'lighthouse' children from Erraid attended Craigh school, walking the whole way there and back in all weathers. No school cars or buses then, yet no harm seemed to have come to the children and Katie McGillivray, who joined them, once told me she could remember only laughs and happy times on that long walk.

The years roll on and I can remember when Katie McGillivray, as an old lady, her life nearing full circle, was taken over at low tide to a nursing home, sitting on her favourite chair, looking bewildered on Hugh Cameron's tractor trailer. Katie never returned and her wish to be buried on her island went unfulfilled. I remember reading about the tragic drowning of her sister-in-law and a shepherd at the pier. I was saddened in more recent times to hear of the death of Christine, but she had her wish to be buried on the island she loved and her name has been carved on a rock near her old home. The Erraid eagles have long gone, there are more visitors and the internet is part of life on Erraid, but in all the years I have been visiting, I have never been so reassured about its future.

The years indeed rush on, but that first visit to Erraid for me, when I managed to 'do a David Balfour' and found myself cut off by the tide, remain clear in my memory. It took a full half-minute to realise I was really trapped. What to do? I decided to climb back to the top of the island to find the rocks which were David's observation point and provided him with some shelter. I grinned a little wryly to myself at my foolishness because the last thing I wanted was an uncomfortable night in the open in the rain. It was David Balfour weather again with a vengeance. The wind began to gust and the rain flew horizontally. The sea on the west shore was roaring. The difference between David and me, in our separate plights, however, was that David arrived soaked and stayed soaked, I arrived more or less dry and had the means to stay that way.

Modern climbing and walking gear, of course, has changed out of all recognition. Climbers and hikers nowadays would snigger at my 1960s outdoor attire. 'Antique' would be their kindest comment and, unlike today, it gave absolutely no acknowledgement to fashion. It was all that was available, however, and I cross-matched it merrily with my old army effects. They gave me a certain crumpled, often-slept-in-ditches appearance, but all my climbing friends cut the same sartorial dash. We didn't care because we didn't know any better.

My army camouflage jacket was windproof rather than waterproof, so I pulled out my old groundsheet that served also as a poncho and swung it on. I wore anorak windproof trousers and over these, with the rain drumming, I pulled a pair of light waterproofs. From a side pocket of my rucksack I produced my trusty, long-superannuated cap that once was recognisable as cavalry twill. In high winds its peak kept my anorak hood from flapping uncomfortably about my ears. I should say a word about that cap. It had served me well in a variety of other uses like wiping up around camp fires. It was utterly disreputable and something of a joke among my friends. Once on a ferry to Skye I was reluctantly persuaded to bid it a ceremonial farewell. I cast my beloved cap to the dark waters, but the wind caught it and returned it like a boomerang almost to my hand. After that I regarded it as my 'lucky cap' and I was glad of it on Erraid.

I could not find David's flat-topped rock and I settled for jamming myself between two large boulders lower down. I collected several washed-up planks and made a rough roof with these and bits of rope and an old hessian sack, but I could see it was going to be a long, wet night, with the rain swirling and trickling down my neck. There would be a low tide about midnight, I reckoned, and I could use it to step over to the mainland. I would still have to find somewhere to spend the night, I thought, and stumbling across the Ross of Mull terrain in darkness would make me a bigger fool.

I decided to have a last look at David Balfour's island before darkness fell. The wind was high now, perhaps not a gale, but fierce enough to elicit a series of noise responses from the crannies and sharp edges of the rocks around me that sounded like groans and little screams and low moans. I trudged and scrambled from Erraid Sound on the north of the islet, by Rub ha Calachain point, above Balfour's Bay, to the Tinker's Hole (or Fiddler's Hole as Stevenson called it) on the south shore. It was blowing wild. The waves dashing on Erraid's seaward rocks were like wild things roaring, yelled my imagination. Steady on! I said to myself. I remembered, too, Erraid in legend was home to the sea-witch, Kirsteen McVurich, the victim of a Silkie seal, and down by the shore I thought I heard her cackle. A light was on in Katie McGillivray's house and that cheered me up. That little, yellow gleam looked inviting and I could almost feel the heat from her stove. She'll be boiling up her cocoa, I thought to myself, but I stayed well clear. The lighthouse keepers' cottages remained in blackness. I was alone on the island, well, just Katie and me – and she didn't know I was there.

In preparing for my trip I had decided not to take a tent. David Balfour found accommodation where he could, clamped down in the heather when night found him if he had to, and so would I. The trick of survival in a climate like Scotland's is the ability to stay dry. In my rucksack I had one complete change of dry clothes. They must stay dry. Walking in wet clothes does no harm so long as you keep on the move. Sitting in wet clothes for any length of time, especially in an icy wind, can do mischief. At the bottom of my rucksack I also had an 'Arctic Special' sleeping bag, not as warm as the best today perhaps, but good enough. The same rules applied: it must stay dry. In the weather both David Balfour and I encountered on Erraid, it was best kept tucked away.

I also had no worries about food. My rations consisted of two pounds of coarse oatmeal to make dramach, a pound of raisins and a pound of thick, pungent, yellow cheese, tea, sugar, some chocolate and boiled sweets. What David Balfour would have given for that meal! Give me my cheese and a cup of sweet, scalding tea and I will walk to

John o' Groats and back, I had said to a friend. In one of my rucksack flaps was my primus stove, my army billycan was near the top and my tin mug hung outside on a strap at the ready. Dramach? It was the main diet of David Balfour and Allan Breck on their wanderings. Dramach is merely oatmeal and cold water stirred to a gooey mess.

I settled into my hard bed, with my rucksack as a pillow. If I squeezed tight against the larger rock only a small portion of me was marginally in the rain. I brewed my tea, threw in another teaspoonful of sugar and tried to think of other things. I must have fallen asleep, too, because I woke with a start. A fiendish, dark face was staring into my eyes. I let out a cry, banged my head on the rock and jumped to my feet. I was just in time to see the long shape of a very startled otter disappear over a small ridge. Poor thing! It, too, must have had the fright of its life. Now I was wide awake and frozen and the top of my

FIGURE 17. It was in this house that the 20-year-old Robert Louis Stevenson lived during his three-week stay on Erraid in 1870. It is still known as the Stevenson House. Nowadays it is used by the Findhorn Community as a storeroom and workshop for making candles. *Alun John*

shirt and jumper were somehow soaked. Instantly I made up my mind. I pulled my things together, heaved my rucksack over one shoulder and groped my way to the lighthouse keepers' cottages.

Was anyone at home? I gave a gentle knock on the first one I came to. It was set back on its own off the street and looked smaller than the others. Again no answer. I turned the handle and stepped inside. A quick fumble into my rucksack and there were my matches, wrapped in a small piece of oilskin and, beside it, the long, new candle I had bought specially for such events. In a minute I had my wet clothes off, hung up, and my sleeping bag out. Luxury! Forty years later I discovered from Paul Johnston the cottage I had chosen that night in the dark was where Robert Louis Stevenson stayed during his time on Erraid. It is still known as the Stevenson House.

In his short story *The Merry Men*, Stevenson paints the kind of storm on the islet that I bless my stars I did not encounter. I never read it without thinking of my own shivering half-night under my rock on the island. The Ben Kyaw he mentioned is Ben More. This is Stevenson's account of bad weather on Erraid and the Findhorn Community people will vouch for its accuracy:

> Now the storm in its might would seize and shake the four
> corners of the roof, roaring like Leviathan in anger. Anon, in a
> lull, cold eddies of tempest moved shudderingly in the room,
> lifting the hair upon our heads and passing between us as we sat.
> And again the wind would break forth in a chorus of melancholy
> sounds, hooting low in the chimney, wailing with flutelike softness
> round the house ... The wind blew the breath out of a man's
> nostrils; all heaven seemed to thunder overhead like a huge sail;
> and where there fell a momentary lull on Aros, we could hear the
> gusts dismally sweeping in the distance. Over all the lowlands of
> the Ross the wind must have blown as fierce as on the open sea;
> and God only knows the uproar that was raging round the head of
> Ben Kyaw ... All round the isle of Aros the surf, with an
> incessant, hammering thunder, beat upon the reefs and beaches.
> Now louder in one place, now lower in another, like the
> combinations of orchestral music, the constant mass of sound
> hardly varied for a moment.

Some storm! By six next morning I was awake and there was hardly a breath of wind. The sky was wall-to-wall dunnock-egg blue, the sun was up and Ben More stood out sharp and proud. That's my target, I thought, that's where David Balfour would make for and it will be my signpost. My map told me the rising smoke David saw while still captive of the island would most likely be towards Bunessan. It's on my way. I hung my wet things out to dry on a wall, munched the last ham sandwich I had bought in Oban and brewed another mug of tea. I climbed back to the hilltop to enjoy the peace once more before I left the island. I sat where I thought David Balfour might have sat, or Robert Louis Stevenson, and let the whole scene wash over me.

When I saw the tide ebb low enough I went back to the Stevenson House and gathered my belongings. Up went the rucksack and I strolled down the path that led past Katie's cottage and towards that corner of the island I now knew would at least be fordable. Katie was outside and I gave her a wave. 'What a fine day!' I called. Katie raised her hand in agreement. I thought: I bet she's saying to herself 'where on earth did he come from?'

As I turned the promontory that leads to the low tide crossing point, I saw – with just a little relief – that I was able to splash over without even getting my feet wet. I stopped for a moment at the other side. 'I'll be back!' I called out loud to Erraid. Then I took the first step of my journey Edinburgh-bound following David Balfour's footsteps.

5

Across Mull

How David Balfour found many tribulations on Mull and
I am puzzled by his route; I hear of a headless horseman,
discover 'White Settlers' thick on the ground, meet the
owner of a castle, share a dram with a Foreign
Legionnaire, keep company with a ghost and find my way
to the Torosay ferry.

If David Balfour tried to tramp across Mull today, the chances are he
would be mown down by a tour bus within half-an-hour. That great,
ragged and dangerous wayside highwayman, the blind catechist
Duncan Mackiegh, whom David encountered near Glen More, would
last barely five minutes. It is all change on Mull today – and who is
to argue that the speed of change in the last 40 years, since I first
marched the *Kidnapped* Way, is not more profound than in the whole
of the previous 200 years?

When I first crossed Mull, rucksack on back, it seemed the island
still retained a powerful grip on its past. Indeed, I remarked to a friend
that the old Highland traditions and island way of life were
reassuringly secure. No commercialism then, poor communications,
few strangers, glorious isolation. How wrong could I be! The drain of
native Mull folk was a process begun in a flood in the middle of the
nineteenth century with the ethnic Clearances and continued at a
faster rate than newcomers arrived. Until now!

I remembered in *Kidnapped* how David described his elderly host
in the cottage where he spent the night near Erraid. David called him
a 'gentleman', quickly adding in parenthesis 'I call him so because of
his manners, for his clothes were falling off his back'. The old
'gentleman' listened to David's tale with great gravity, kindness and
pity, then gave him a bonnet for his head and refused payment. David

FIGURE 18. Mull signpost. From its rocky summit Ben More surveys a harsh
landscape of sea, lochs, barren moors and bald mountains, the home for hoodie
crows and red deer. It was along the foot of Ben More, perhaps following part
of the Pilgrim's Way to Iona, that David Balfour most likely wandered as the
lad with the silver button, trying to find his way to the Torosay ferry. Stevenson
gives few clues to David's exact route on Mull, but this photograph of
Glen More indicates the tough terrain he encountered.

commented: 'If these are the wild Highlanders, I could wish my own
folk wilder'. On that first hike across Mull in 1960, I found the reality
echoed David's words. The people I met along the way were also the
epitome of good manners, hospitable, tolerant, shy – and full of pride
in their island. It seemed to me at the time many spoke Gaelic or had
a grasp of it, in spite of the language being under pressure in what had
been a bastion of Gaeldom.

But that was before the great people movement came to Mull, hand-
in-hand with a culture change so that the accents of Birmingham,
Sheffield, Manchester, the Home Counties, Glasgow and Edinburgh
have muted the Gaelic voices to relative silence.

On stepping off Erraid, my top priority was to decide where I was
going.

Before setting out I had pored over ancient maps of the period looking for the old roads. The difficulty is that David's exact route across Mull is vague. Stevenson knew Mull better than some other sections of the *Kidnapped* Trail, where he provides clear signposts, yet David is left to explain how his off-course wanderings of around 100 miles took him four days to travel the 50 miles 'as the crow flies' from Erraid to Torosay. On that first march, I was not even sure of the location of the Torosay ferry. I scoured a variety of maps searching for the name Torosay, which I understood was an area rather than a particular site, but the only reference I could find was Torosay Castle near Craignure. The castle was not built until 1858, 106 years after David's journey, but at least it was in the right direction. He was making for Kinlochaline, over the Sound of Mull, on the mainland in Morvern, clutching Allan Breck's silver button, and logic suggested the Torosay ferry had to be close to the shortest crossing. One way or another, I guessed I would land up around Fishnish, the site of the modern ferry point, and sensibly the shortest water route.

I decided to put my faith in G. Langlands & Son, Campbeltown, whose map was published on August 1, 1801. Although sparse in detail, it appeared only 49 years after David passed that way. Had David Balfour known about the various tracks available to him, which he did not, his choices, according to Langlands, would have been more or less as follows. A reasonable track led from Fidden Farm, opposite Erraid, by Loch Pottie (today Loch Poit) to Bunessan. Langlands gives no indication of Fionnphort in 1801 or even a road leading directly to Iona. A further track led along the south-coast route from Conarst, in Port nan Ron bay, a little east of Erraid, to Scour (Scoor today), where it headed inland, passed Loch Assapol and the medieval Kilvickeon Church, also to arrive at Bunessan. Okay, first stop Bunessan! But I would take neither of these routes. I would head directly over the hill, as I guessed David would have done, in the general direction of Ben More, towards the chimney smoke both David and I had seen from Erraid.

I splashed off the islet and headed up the brae opposite in great good spirits. Edinburgh, here I come, I said to myself, and whistled a few bars of 'Johnny Cope' just to please Allan Breck. I had hardly been on my way 10 minutes when I met up with Hugh Cameron, who farmed Knockvoligan, just above David's island.

'My guess is David Balfour would have followed the Pilgrim's Way along the side of Loch Scridain to the entrance of Glen More,' Hugh considered. 'Stevenson would have taken that route when he was on Mull. It was the most used road then, and surely he would have wanted David Balfour to follow in his own footsteps. After Glen More, who can tell which way David went?'

That was a helpful start. Truth to tell, all views I could muster were helpful at that time.

The ground across that part of the Ross is low-lying by Mull standards, but pocked by huge granite outcrops, bogs, gullies, clumps of wild bramble, heather and bracken, then small oases of cropped meadow, sparkling with wild flowers, followed by stretches of treacherous tussocky grass that makes each step awkward and ankle-wrenching. Within a few strides I knew my journey would not be done at speed.

I struck the main Iona road about a mile short of Bunessan. Half-a-mile on I came upon a young man taking road measurements. I bade him a jolly good day as I passed. He looked up and, my goodness, I knew him! His name was James Pattison, and he had been a few years ahead of me at Breadalbane Academy in Aberfeldy. I had not seen him for around six years and much had happened to both of us since then. Amazing! Small country Scotland, but I considered this wayside meeting remarkable and fortuitous.

I could not have fallen in with better company. As I recollect, working as a road engineer on Mull was Jim's first job and he was enjoying it immensely. I could see he was under Mull's spell and he treated me to a eulogy of the people, the landscape, the wilderness, the wildlife, island tradition, music and Mull sunsets. I remember how horrified he was at the thought of my sleeping out that night (and there was I thinking nothing of it), and so I was persuaded to stay with his landlady, a Mrs McDonald, at the top of the village, where I was introduced to her husband, a factor to the Duke of Argyll. David Balfour had a roof over his head that first night – and so should I.

Jim was fascinated by my *Kidnapped* project. 'David would go through Glen More,' he felt certain. 'It was a recognised route and part of the Pilgrim's Way to Iona. It would have appealed to Stevenson, too, because of its desolation. It's a wild, dreich place full of hoodie crows waiting to pick your bones,' said Jim cheerily.

'No, you're wrong,' interrupted Mr McDonald. 'Surely David would have gone through Glen Forsa. Fishnish or thereabouts has to be the Torosay ferry. The Glen Forsa route would take him there.'

As I had done many times in other places, we had a good argument about David Balfour's Mull wanderings.

Even at that time, Jim was expressing what he called his apprehensions about Mull's future. 'I'm seeing small changes already,' he said. 'They'll get bigger and faster. The old order is under pressure. Tradition versus new thinking. A different kind of people with different ideas and aspirations are arriving. Once the roads are better and tourism is more developed, there will be more and more change. I hope the local folk can cope. I wouldn't want to see them hurt – and I hope Mull is not the loser.'

But change doesn't have to be negative, I countered. It can surely be for the better? Better communications, more contact with the rest of Scotland, more jobs, different jobs, more money coming in, improved housing, more entertainment, less isolation, a better quality of life.

'Maybe' was all he would say.

The following day, as I left Bunessan, and headed out along the road that skirts the long sea arm of Loch Scridain, I passed the little primary school on top of the hill. A handful of small boys were chasing sheep out of the playground so they could play football. Those stunning Mull vistas were all around. I saw the headteacher, Mr Robbie, talking to one of the children. On impulse I walked in and said hello. Mr Robbie told me the school had around 26 pupils then, but the roll was dropping fast and it had just lost its Junior High School status. He was rather depressed about it. Some of the children still spoke Gaelic, but they, too, were becoming fewer with every year that passed. Today, after a number of amalgamations, the school roll is healthily in the mid-40s, going well and there are three teachers – but no Gaelic speakers.

Marching along the edge of Loch Scridain was a joy. The road was narrow and hard-soft, which meant not particularly well made up, with grass verges easy on the feet. Cars were few and there seemed as many lorries and vans, but occasionally only, pulling over at the passing places, giving each other a wave. Sometimes they sat two abreast, chatting to each other for ten minutes on end, then with a couple of toots they were on their way again, and they would give me a wave, too. People were less frequent. Changed days, I thought, because up to almost the middle of the nineteenth century, before the Clearances, Mull's population was around 10,000, and that was the Mull David Balfour knew.

I gazed at the passing scene round-eyed. Even the place names on that first march sounded poetic to me: Ardtun, Ardchnishnish (a hard one that), Coillenangabhar, Clachan Falbhain, Ormsaig, Torban, Killinaig, Pennycross and Pennyghael. Wonderful! As Loch Scridain unfolded on my left, always ahead was Ben More, and a range of mountains and glens all the way to the big tops of Beinn Talaidh and Dun da Ghaoithe. And across the loch, the huge cathedral-like cliffs of Burgh. A glance over my shoulder, and further filmset panoramas of loch and wilderness were revealed where I had just been.

It can never be quite the same again. In springtime nowadays the tour buses are already negotiating the hairpins, the humpy bridges and blind corners. In summer it is full-scale invasion. I am all for sharing Mull, but folk in cars and buses comfortably at their air-conditioned ease, gazing at Mull's passing wonders through polished glass, inhabit an insulated, unreal colour-calendar world and I sometimes feel sorry for what they are not seeing. But to be out on the open road, with the wind in your hair, the tangle in your nose, a thousand sounds from the hill and the loch below, and to speak to the folk at the roadside is a hiker's heaven. And on Loch Scridain, as I tramped on, those tour bus travellers would have missed the merganser, the big grey seal on the rock, the goldeneyes, eiders and shelducks, the heron snatching his fish tea and the carrion crow breaking a peewit's egg on a stone with 17 robbed shells scattered around it. I did not see an eagle that first visit, although I have seen many since, and nowadays the re-introduced sea eagles can also float into view, white tails spread as they ride the air currents.

I had Glen More in mind as my target for the day. I reckoned it would be around 15 miles. From the Loch Scridain approach the Glen More entrance is dramatic. Conifer plantations are at either end now, and a two-car-wide, smooth-as-glass highway slices through it, but on that first hike Glen More was bare, treeless, lonely, a high and hostile place, with Ben More's bleak face rising above. A car passed as I contemplated shelter for the night. It navigated the ruts tenderly, and

I could hear the swish of the reeds growing in the middle of the road as the vehicle passed over them. Sections of that old road are still there and I remember thinking it had been laid across deep peat, with fingers crossed that it didn't sink out of sight.

The roofless, ruined cottage at Derrynaculen, in the mouth of the glen, looks hardly welcoming, but it commands a splendid prospect over the Ross, the walls are wind-breakers and it was perfect for my needs. I estimated it was around here that David Balfour encountered the blind highwayman Duncan Mackiegh. There is a trick for sleeping rough – dress up for the occasion. That means put on more clothes. One of my prized possessions for such situations was a thick climber's jumper that had defied the rules of washing. Instead of shrinking it grew bigger. It reached almost to my knees and the arms were a third longer than the original. When the chill set in, I could draw it over my head and almost crawl inside. A second pair of socks pulled up to my knees and I was as cosy in my sleeping bag as in a bed at the Dorchester.

Time to consider routes again. On that first trip I decided to take the easy option and go right through Glen More. At the time it seemed Torosay Castle was a sensible place to ask directions for the Torosay ferry. I considered that if David Balfour had wandered far off his path, but kept to the existing tracks of the day, then according to Langlands he could conceivably have tramped down Glen Leidle from Pennyghael to Karsaig (Carsaig now), although the road was not marked then. However, a road was indicated from Carsaig along the coast, also used by pilgrims, to Loch Buie and continued to the head of Loch Spelve. It eventually carried on to Tayunrubich (Lochdonhead now), Achnacrosh (Achnacroish now), more or less the site of Torosay Castle, Craiganure (Craignure now although it is still pronounced the old way it was spelt) and eventually on to Fishnish. Perhaps a more likely road for David Balfour, also shown by Langlands, ran from Loch Buie up Gleann a Chaiginn Mhor by the chain of dark lochs in that dark glen – Airdeglais, below the crag of the eagle, Crun Lochan and Loch Sgunbain. This track cut directly across Glen More at Torness, then down Glen Forsa to Pennygown and the Torosay ferry.

I puzzled these routes for years, and at one time or another I have now traversed them all. Time and time again I checked through my copy of *Kidnapped* to see if it would divulge further clues to David's route. Nothing. In those early days, however, I didn't know there was a Stevenson map! If I had known of its existence earlier, I could have saved myself some blisters, although I would have missed some magnificent country. On the other hand, Stevenson was deliberately vague about Mull, and these detours could indeed have reflected David's meanderings.

It is interesting to note that the map for *Kidnapped* was produced in the same office as the map for *Treasure Island*. RLS's cousin, David A. Stevenson, had joined the family business as the fifth Stevenson to serve the Northern Lighthouse Board, and RLS gave him detailed instructions for his *Kidnapped* map. As explained in the Foreword to *Kidnapped*, it was always a 'probable' route. Where David and Allan Breck wandered off course or took evasive action to avoid the red soldiers, RLS instructed the route should be drawn imprecisely as a wavering, dotted line. RLS was out of luck with his maps: the original *Treasure Island* map was lost by the publisher, and had to be reinvented, much to RLS's annoyance; some of his directions for *Kidnapped* seem to have been ignored by David Stevenson's drawing office. It may have been that Stevenson, writing from Bournemouth, provided a small-scale map, which would have made it almost impossible to show the proposed wanderings in detail. Whatever the reason, all along the way, dotted or full, the line is direct, unwavering and only partially helpful because in some areas it even departs from the *Kidnapped* text.

The small-scale *Kidnapped* map, however, follows more or less my route to the head of Loch Scridain. David also entered Glen More as I did, but then appears to turn up Glen Forsa at Torness, between Beinn Talaidh on the left and that range of big tops on the right, Sgurr Dearg, Dun da Ghaoithe, Beinn Mheadhoin and Beinn Chreagach Mhor. After that it is a pleasant hike of about seven miles down the burn, then along the banks of the River Forsa to Pennygown and what is Mull's little airport today. Aeroplanes! They would have had David Balfour's eyes popping. The Stevenson map indicates the Torosay ferry ran from this point, which is possible, depending on the currents, but more likely it sailed from Fishnish, and there were criss-cross tracks over Glen Forsa that could have delivered David directly to the ferry.

In fact, although this whole area was high and wild, there were several old drove roads off Glen More that David could have taken.

FIGURE 19. Just a pile of stones by the old roadside ... but it marks the burial place in Glen More of pedlar John Jones, who died a local hero here in 1891. On his rounds, John found two families ravaged by smallpox, with their neighbours too scared to help. The stricken families would have died, but John took care of them until they were on the mend. Sadly, John caught the dreaded disease himself, and died where he fell near the River Lussa.

If Stevenson knew of the drove road that ran from Holly Tree Fank, by Allt Teanga Brideig, to the Mam Clachaig or up over the Mam Choireadail, David might even have followed in Columba's footsteps. In the old days, despite the harshness of terrain and elements, much walking was done between north and south Torosay, horses were in constant use, either as pack animals or to haul the fleeds (sledges), and at one time mail was carried trans-Glen More by a postie on horse-back. Torness was once the site of an annual horse market in August, and some of the old buildings are still visible. This is the main gateway to Glen Forsa, the landscape now softened by an unexpected forestry plantation, which wasn't there when I first marched the route, and irritatingly not only bars the ancient entrance but covers part of the old track.

If you are unlucky (or lucky if you believe in ghosts) and hear the sound of a galloping horse around these parts as night falls, look carefully because it may be the headless Eoghain a Chin Bhig, Ewan of the Little Head, riding out from his former fortified home at Loch Sgunbain. Warrior Ewan was decapitated in battle when he challenged his father, John MacLean, Lord of Loch Buie, back in the Middle Ages. His men fled down Glen More towards Loch Scridain, but the vengeful father caught up with them near Craig and massacred the lot. It is said the headless Ewan makes an appearance around Moy Castle when there is a MacLean death.

As I passed through Glen More, I wondered at the hardiness of those people of old who traversed such a place. David Balfour gives a description of them as he crossed the Ross: 'Some went bare, only for a hanging coat or great-coat, and carried their trousers on their backs like a useless burthen; some had made an imitation of the tartan with little parti-coloured stripes patched together like an old wife's quilt; others, again, still wore the highland philabeg, but by putting a few stitches between the legs, transformed it into a pair of trousers like a Dutchman's. All those makeshifts were condemned and punished, for the law was harshly applied, in hope to break up the clan spirit; but in that out-of-the-way, sea-bound isle, there were few to make remarks and fewer to tell tales. They seemed in great poverty; which was no doubt natural, now that the rapine was put down, and the chiefs kept no longer an open house ...'

I tried to visualise these folk against that vast Glen More setting. Stevenson made no reference to the landscape here, but Glen More is high, mighty and pitiless, intimidating for the weary, and downright dangerous when the big blizzards blow in winter. It does not have the rocky drama of Glencoe, but in my mind I place Glen More equal to Glencoe for scale and majesty.

My aim was to reach Craignure by the end of the day. I came by the back way through the grounds of David Bryce's Scottish Baronial pile of Torosay Castle, and parked my rucksack at the front door. Now I was glad I had shaved that morning in a burn at Derrynaculen. A gentleman came up behind me and introduced himself as Colonel Geoffrey Miller, owner of Torosay, and asked if he could help. I explained I was following David Balfour's footsteps and was about 200 years late in trying to catch the Torosay ferry. Could he tell me exactly where the ferry was located? That caught him off guard, but he felt sure David Balfour could well have come this way because the Stevensons knew the Castle and had once published a paper on the unusual tides at Craignure. As for the ferry, well, it might have been at Craignure, but more likely it was up at Fishnish or Salen, and we discussed the route over a cup of tea.

Has anyone ever counted the rooms in Torosay Castle? There must be at least 50 and the estate runs to 24,000 acres. The place is huge and kept in immaculate condition along with its manicured grounds. Indeed, it was the same Colonel Miller, and his wife Mrs Guthrie-James, who began the heroic battle to save the castle from falling into dereliction. At one time there were not enough buckets available to catch the drips coming through the roof. The castle even became a commercial enterprise for a period as the Tangle of the Isles Hotel. The remarkable Guthrie family have owned Torosay since Arbuthnott Guthrie rashly bought it after he lost in love in competition with his brother around 1860. Theirs is a family story of adventure, travel, big business and dedication to a home they clearly adore. Their castle has now been thrown open to the public.

I strolled down to Craignure, surely half its size then. The ancient Craignure Inn remains unchanged, and years later I had an interesting experience there with a ghost. Billy McGregor is mine host these days, Billy with shoulders wide as a barn, and the same Billy who was a Foreign Legionnaire and a special forces veteran of the Falklands War.

We shared a dram across his bar and talked about ghosts. Like me he doesn't believe in them. Yet he can't explain the apparition of the elderly lady some of his guests see from time to time. He admits, reluctantly, the vision has even appeared to him. I scoffed at this suggestion and spoke of a trick of the light. Believe me, there are no ghosts, I said, and went back to the hotel lounge where I had left my wife on her own reading a book. She said the strangest thing had just happened. A potted plant on a table on the other side of the room had sudddenly thrown itself on the floor, spilling earth all over the carpet. It had happened a few seconds before I entered the room, exactly at the time I was stating to Billy McGregor I didn't believe in ghosts. How do you explain that?

FIGURE 20. The Craignure Inn is an ancient island tryst and boasts a ghost. Today the inn remains a popular evening meeting spot for locals and visitors, and the proceedings are watched over by mine host, the broad-shouldered Billy McGregor, former Foreign Legionnaire and special forces veteran of the Falklands War. There is never trouble at his inn. *Alun John*

When I walked through the Craignure of 1960, I noticed the MacBrayne's steamer, the *Loch Earn*, standing off from the village. No pier was big enough to take it then and a small boat ferried out goods and passengers. It was just about to leave.

'Where's it headed?' I called to the ferryman.

'Salen,' came the reply. 'I'll let ye on if ye sign my petition for a new pier.'

On the spur of the moment I decided to hop aboard. The ferryman told me his name was George Clyne. He explained great things could happen at Craignure if only they had a pier able to take the big ferries from Oban. Cars, lorries and tour buses could then land at Craignure, he said. Just imagine! I signed with pleasure and was taken out to the *Loch Earn* and exchanged for several rolls of wire netting, a sheepdog in a crate and two big boxes for Torosay Castle.

'I hope you get your pier soon,' I shouted to George, in his wee boat below, and he stuck up a thumb. I have often wondered since if my signature helped long-term to improve Mull's economy or whether I was assisting in the destruction of a way of life.

The years passed, the pier arrived along with the visitor hordes, but the cars and buses trundle off the Oban ferry and tend to keep on trundling to spread their tourist gold in other corners of the island. And now the accents of Kent, Yorkshire, Lancashire, Lothian and Lanarkshire, instead of retreating homewards with the first nip of winter, remain thick on the ground. The visitors came, saw, liked what they saw, and decided to put down roots. Who can blame them? Mull is one of the most beautiful places I know. Now, however, there are a great, great many non-Mull accents throughout the island. Some locals say there are lots and lots too many, probably more than on any other major Scottish island. Some call them the 'White Settlers' behind their backs. Understandably, these newcomers want to improve things, and bring to Mull some aspects of the way of life and culture they enjoyed at home.

Unlike the wandering Scots, who left their homeland for economic reasons or were forced out, some at bayonet point, or had their homes burned, also largely for economic reasons, the newcomers have come in search of the improved quality of life Mull offers. No one goes to Mull to become a millionaire. But for local folk many of the newcomers could just as well be millionaires because indigenous Mull

people tend to be outbid, outpriced and out-thought by this new
section of the island community whose commercial instincts have been
honed in big cities and who are accustomed to getting their way. The
process is called 'progress'. From Columba to the Vikings to
nineteenth-century landowners who saw the value of sheep rather than
people, Mull is not unfamiliar with incomers who brought change. Yet
from today's perspective, it is sad to see old Mull, a fragile heritage
and people now, in danger of being overwhelmed.

It is a world removed from Knockvoligan, that little croft on the
top of the hill opposite Erraid. There John Cameron, his wife Mary,
from Iona, took over from his dad Hugh, whom I met on the trail of
David Balfour so many years earlier. John as a child lived on Erraid
in the little Stevenson-built house down by the pier. John and Mary
are part of the Mull farming heritage, dedicated, motivated, genuine
and wondering what the future holds. Blackface sheep make no easier
living on Mull now than they did in his father's time, and John notices
little change in his family fortunes, his lifestyle or the hours he works.
There are never enough hours.

The late Alasdair 'Attie' MacKechnie, from Fionnphort, a knowl-
edgeable local historian of Mull past and present, a native Gaelic
speaker, and a true gentleman by the David Balfour definition,
brought perspective to bear. 'Many of the changes are for the good,'
said Attie. 'But some are maybe not the Mull way. We're not a pushy
people and sometimes our voices go unheard. City folk naturally herd
together. They're used to city ways. The wide open spaces and solitary life on Mull has never bothered us. We quite like it that way. But
we should never forget the reason for the empty spaces or the people
who once inhabited them. There are some of the new Mull folk who
have been good for the island and bring fresh ideas with them
and they fit in easily; and some easier than others. And some can
never fit in.'

I met a young woman who had just left school and was about to
take her place as a student at Edinburgh University. She was the
daughter of a newcomer family. They had come to Mull from the
English Black Country to give their offspring a better chance. Now
her ambition was to escape from Mull as fast as she could. Everything
she wanted to do with her life was outside the island, she said. Her
parents felt they had found their true home on Mull. They considered

themselves Mull people. In the twenty-first century it remains a situation that is a familiar, auld sang in the islands – indeed in Scotland – and echoes sadly across centuries.

I spent the night in a wood outside Salen 40 years ago. I turned in early because it had been a long day, at least a 20-mile slog, I guessed, and I wanted an early start in the morning. All my thoughts were on the next day following the lad with the silver button across the Torosay ferry. But had I considered the future then, not in my wildest imaginings would I have foreseen the changes to Mull 40 years down the road. Had I done so, I might not have slept so easily.

6

The House Beyond Kingairloch

How the lad with the silver button crossed the Torosay ferry and spent a vile night at Kinlochaline, I meet the present-day ferryman, hear of a romance, lunch with a lady minister, march a road soon to vanish, go to church, and conclude that cheese and raisins beat dramach any day.

I heard the hunting buzzard as I walked up the side of the River Aline. Sometimes I caught sight of him in slothful flight, sometimes he disappeared from view, but that wild and plaintive shriek always gave away his whereabouts. A little beyond Claggan, where the main road swings right at Strath Uladail, I sat down among the trees near the burn to study the map and my notes from the maps of two centuries ago. After this point, I would be venturing out on the open moor and I wanted to be certain of my route across what would be rough, desolate and exposed country.

The Highlanders of old were not daft. If they couldn't reach their destination by boat, they took the land line of least resistance, up glens, rivers, burns or folds in the hills, keeping steep climbs to a minimum. In David's time, according to my 1801 Langlands map, the track through Morvern made the long upward haul from Kinlochaline, in the Allt Beitheach basin, probably keeping to the firmer ground on the flank of Beinn Chlaonleud. The one-car-wide B8043 today, which takes a sharp right before the main road descends to meet Loch Sunart, follows David's ancient track to Kingairloch almost precisely. In fact, there were many other less formal routes, detours and pathways David could have followed. The track by Loch Tearnait, down Glen Sanda and along the coast to Kingairloch, was an obvious alternative. Stevenson would be familiar with the old maps of the area, and the route he chose for David, copied into the *Kidnapped* map, follows

FIGURES 21 AND 22. When David Balfour made his crossing to Kinlochaline 250 years ago on the Torosay ferry, the passengers took turns on the oars and sang Gaelic boat songs to keep the rhythm. Today the modern Torosay ferry is the Caledonian MacBrayne's *Loch Fyne*, which can deposit 36 cars on the far shore in 20 minutes. In David's day, the skipper was Neil Roy Macrob, and his counterpart today is boatmaster Callum McKechnie, a Jura man with vast experience of the fickle waters around the Hebrides. *Alun John*

Langlands via the north side of Loch Uisge. Good. I had my bearings, so to speak, and felt confident that even if the mist came down, I couldn't go far wrong, not with a main road beside me. I put away the maps, lay back and surveyed the scene.

The buzzard alighted on the dead branch of a fallen tree not 30 yards away. I remained perfectly still. He may not have the size and nobility of the eagle and appears unexcitingly brown from a distance, but close up the adult male is still a handsome chap, dressed in brown, gold and black, with flashes of white, blue-black hooked beak, sharp, dark eye, barred tail, yellow legs and dark talons. He too remained perfectly still, except for his head, which he cocked frequently. I held my breath. The buzzard's eye fixed on something out of my sight in the grass below. As far as I could tell, he was entirely unaware of his audience. Then his body tensed and suddenly he landed on the ground with a plop, wings half spread, looking around, and holding something in the grass with one large set of fishhooks. In that precise second I became aware of two things: a face in a clump of nearby bracken and simultaneously a streak of red as a big dog fox struck the buzzard. The fox seemed to dive on the buzzard, pinning it there, but also gripped its neck or body – difficult to tell which in the hurly-burly – and shook the big raptor. There was a scatter of feathers, the buzzard's wings beat frantically, hitting the ground hard as it tried to take off. For a moment the fox was below the buzzard and I could see those big talons scratch the air.

My goodness! I could hardly believe my eyes. It had all happened so quickly and without warning. Maybe I should have sat still to watch the drama played out. Instead, I leapt to my feet and ran forward, instinctively wanting to save the buzzard. Immediately the fox let go, ran down the burn and disappeared. And then there he was again, going up the opposite side, red brush stuck out straight. He even stopped for a moment at the top of the far bank to take a last look in my direction, cheeky-like, before vanishing for good. The buzzard was badly injured, but after a few minutes it managed to fly up into the trees, landing clumsily among the top branches. It remained there silently for 20 minutes or so, then was able to flop and glide over the trees and out of my view. Whether it survived or not is speculation.

Here was ruthless, raw nature striking like a thunderbolt. I remember telling the late David Stephen, a naturalist friend who had witnessed most things in the wilds, but this was outside his experience. He had seen a fox lift a pheasant sitting on eggs while he tried to photograph it, and a fox take a feeding mallard from a burn, but never a fox tackle a buzzard. There were probably hungry cubs nearby, he guessed. It is an experience I will not forget.

I had come over to the mainland from Mull on an early ferry from Fishnish to Lochaline. This is the shortest route and close enough to the line David Balfour took on the Torosay ferry. There were several old piers in this area and one is still visible a hundred yards below the present ferry point. A mudflat is also close by, which could well be where David Balfour's Torosay ferry was beached, beside handy rocks or a pile of stones because passengers would no more want their feet wet then than now. The skipper in David's day was Neil Roy Macrob, a clansman of Allan Breck, and therefore someone David could trust. The ferry was crowded when he made the one-and-a-half mile crossing, short enough you may think, but a slow, hard pull in those days, with the weather and currents notoriously fickle. The passengers, mostly MacLeans, helped the crew on the oars and struck up Gaelic boat-songs to keep the rhythm. It was in the mouth of Loch Aline they heard the heart-rending wailing from the emigrant ship bound for the colonies. The shore was crowded with families and friends, and little skiffs ran back and forward in final farewells. The people on the ship sang 'Lochaber No More' and the tears were running freely.

Neil Roy's counterpart today is Callum McKechnie, skipper of Caledonian MacBrayne's ferry, the *Loch Fyne*, which plied the Kyle of Lochalsh-Kyleakan run to Skye until the new bridge made it redundant. Neil Roy would be thunderstruck today by the modern ferry and the changes all around. Not just by roads, cars, lorries and tour buses, but by the fact that his Torosay ferry can now take up to 36 cars at a time, and deposit them with precision and at speed in 20 minutes or thereabouts. As I recollect, when I first used the Torosay ferry its capability was six cars.

Neil and Callum are two of a breed, Hebridean seamen, weaned on these particular waters, who know their idiosyncrasies, changing voices, and respect their might. Callum is a Jura man with a lifetime's experience in these parts. It matters not whether a crossing is long or short, the size of craft large or small: taking accountability for the lives of people in Hebridean waters is serious. It is not everyone who can take that kind of responsibility. Nor is it merely a matter of technical training, although it is that, too, but mostly it is about seamanship, instinct, knowing the vessel, knowing the patch, understanding seaspeak, knowing everything relevant, being able to act accordingly, and taking no chances.

Callum has seen Force 10s and 11s roaring down the Sound of Mull, spume flying, or the sea springing into a rage out of nothing. Scotland's west-coast waters can be moody and cantankerous, and the wind can take it into its head to challenge the unsuspecting without warning and for no reason. Big north-westers are trouble, but when Callum decides it is too chancy to take the ferry out, which is rarely, it is final. No argument. It is a decision that can be his alone. For seamen like Neil Roy and Callum, and even Captain Hoseason of the brig *Covenant*, for that matter, their vessels come high in their affections. They don't speak much about it, but it is something felt, and because people and professional reputations are at stake, their boats or ships are one of the most important loves in their lives.

That same breed is being continued in the McKechnie family. Callum's son Ian is also the relief boatmaster, as they term it nowadays, of the back-up crew, and even the young 'deckie' assistant, Gavin Cameron, had a grandfather – another Ian – who was a skipper on that same Fishnish-Lochaline crossing. I noticed one of the crew was an attractive young woman, dressed for the weather, and I asked if she ever nurtured ambitions of being the first female boatmaster of the *Loch Fyne*. No, said Heather Brown, without hesitation, it would conflict with her other plans. Her other plans were to marry Ian McKechnie. They had just become engaged.

The Torosay ferry in David's day took him to Kinlochaline at the head of the loch because the village of Lochaline did not exist then. The pier or beaching place was probably near the river's mouth on the Ardtornish estate, but when I later studied the map published in early editions of *Kidnapped* I discovered a discrepancy between text and the drawn route. The map clearly lands David at a point between Fiunary and Killundine on the mainland, then indicates he walked overland to Kinlochaline in a firm line. This was surely a mistake or misunderstanding in the drawing office and the fastidious Stevenson would not have been pleased. The advice given by Neil Macrob was that David should spend the night in the Kinlochaline Inn, then head next day for Kingairloch, and the ferries at Corran and Ballachulish, where he should ask for the house of James of the Glen. Morvern is blessed by nature along the coast, but remains wild and lonely in the interior. 'The sea in all this part runs deep into the mountains and winds about their roots,' David recounted. 'It makes the country strong to hold and difficult to travel, but full of prodigious wild and dreadful prospects.' As for me, I was looking forward to encountering them.

That Kinlochaline Inn received from David the worst publicity ever penned. It was 'the most beggarly vile place that ever pigs were styed in, full of smoke, vermin, and silent Highlanders', according to David. 'I had not been half-an-hour at the inn (standing in the door most of the time, to ease my eyes from the peat smoke) when a thunderstorm came close by, the springs broke in a little hill on which the inn stood, and one end of the house became a running water. Places of public entertainment were bad enough all over Scotland in those days; yet it was a wonder to myself, when I had to go from the fireside to the bed where I slept, wading over the shoes.'

There is no inn as such at Kinlochaline today, but the little Lochaline Hotel is the oldest at the present ferry point. Mercifully it bears no resemblance to David's overnight bed-with-paddling-pool. As well as local Highlanders, who did not seem particularly silent, and workmen with job projects in the area, its clientèle today includes German, French, Japanese, Italian and Belgian visitors, as well as being a popular haunt for divers. Galleons lie at the bottom of Tobermory Bay and near Duart Castle, and there is a hundred feet of water off the old pier. The deep water attracts monster skate and I was fascinated to watch sea anglers using balloons to take their lines out on the wind and then shoot them down with airguns.

I have stayed over in the Lochaline Hotel on a number of occasions, notably once when I missed the last ferry. Mine host these days is Charlie Lamont, a Glencoe man, who is carrying out improvements. I told him I had known several proprietors over the years, and in my possession is a rare bottle of Lochaline Hotel wine. I don't know if the content is rare, but the label shows a drawing of the Lochaline Hotel. It was gifted to me by a previous owner, Michael Slowick, to drink a toast to Robert Louis Stevenson, if I ever got round to writing a book about the *Kidnapped* Trail.

Lochaline was not founded until around 1830, by local landowner John Sinclair, but the loch has been an important natural harbour since early days. The remains of ancient castles seen on almost every strategic promontory down the Sound of Mull are reminders of those harsh times of blood and onslaught when the MacDonald Lords of the Isles ruled. The fearsome Somerled defeated Viking invaders at the head of Glen Geall, on David Balfour's route, a few miles above the loch. It is believed Columba came this way and the beautiful little church at the top of the village, with its splendid views, springs from Cill Choluimchille, 'the cell of Colm of the churches'. There are vast forests all around Lochaline, and I remember when a shortage of male labour forced local women to take on some of the lighter forestry work. I dubbed them Lochaline's 'lumberjills' in a newspaper headline. Some of these ladies at the time found the headline neither apt nor amusing and informed me of their joint displeasure. They will be grannies now and I apologise to them.

When David Balfour set out from Kinlochaline, he overtook a 'little, stout, solemn man, walking very slowly with his toes turned out, reading a book, and dressed decently and plainly in something of a clerical style'. He was Mr Henderland, a catechist, sent out by that pillar of respectability, the Edinburgh Society for Propagating Christian Knowledge. There is no catechist in Lochaline today, at least as far as I am aware, but the Church of Scotland minister, I felt, would at least share Mr Henderland's religious enthusiasms. I sought out the Rev. Ann Winning, minister of that wee kirk on the vantage point looking over the Sound of Mull. Small world again! Ann turned out to have been a former assistant teacher of English at Breadalbane Academy in Aberfeldy, but long after my time, before she received the call. Of course, she knew all about Stevenson and *Kidnapped* and David Balfour's wanderings, and over lunch in the manse we specu-lated on his possible onward route from Lochaline, and the changes in Scotland then and now.

In the Highlands it can take suspicious decades before incomers are accepted, and that goes for ministers, too, particularly for a woman minister. It was not easy for Ann Winning to break into a tight Highland presbytery, with 'auld lichts' deep set in the auld ways and traditionally male dominated. Simply by being herself, of course, eventually won over doubters, and a little tact and diplomacy helped.

Her parishioners were never a problem. For another less dedicated and caring woman it could have been unfortunate. The Rev. Ann has been in Lochaline for approaching 20 years now and was described to me as 'the genuine article', which is a very great compliment to pay any person.

During that time Lochaline traditionalists have had plenty of opportunity to become accustomed to change. The same people movement I discovered in Mull also declared itself loudly in Morvern. Incomers, as one old resident put it, are everywhere. But there are newcomers – and then there are different newcomers. Some espouse local culture, interests and causes, quickly becoming 'locals', and only their accents give them away. Some fight integration and either try to alter things into what they see as a 'better' way – but not necessarily the Morvern way – which often bears close resemblance to the life they knew elsewhere. Some realise after 18 months and a winter that they have made a mistake and leave. As in Mull, some have brought energy and positive new ideas into the community, but some prefer to remain 'foreigners', living in Morvern but not of it, reluctant to be involved. Some few become over-zealous but with scant appreciation and little interest in what has gone before.

That emigrant ship David Balfour encountered in the mouth of the loch in reality was one of many, although Stevenson used his writer's licence to translate the incident backwards a few years in history to make a point. Morvern was at the heart of the Highland Clearances and Stevenson was a natural supporter of the underdog. In the end it came down to a case of people versus sheep. The sheep won. The people were vanquished. The nearby 'lost' Cameron community of Inniemore is an example of the cruelty inflicted by some landowners on the Morvern people. Fifty men, women and children were evicted at swordpoint in Inniemore in 1824, and their houses set alight to make way for the sheep. 'Highland Mary' Cameron was there and told her story to a minister in the 1860s of how she, her husband and children watched their homes burn. The families were put in boats; some went to Glasgow, others to Canada. 'On the day of leaving Inniemore, I thought my heart would break,' said Mary Cameron. The foundations of the Inniemore homes became overgrown and eventually forgotten. Then a few years ago, the ruined walls were discovered, the story was retold, and the stones now serve as a reminder of an infamous Highland 'ethnic cleansing'.

In good weather, the road to Kingairloch is a pleasure to walk and not simply because it is downhill after the long haul. Once past Loch Uisge, the road is like a ribbon cast into the wind, snaking and twisting as it makes its way to the Abhainn na Coinnich gorge. The old track, in David's day, would follow the burn more closely as it tumbled down the hillside before reaching the flat ground at Kingairloch House, where it then skirted Loch a' Choire and came over the saddle of Ceanna Mor to the tiny community of Camas na Croise.

When I first marched down that road, it was a day to savour. Almost windless, sun high, and I was in shirt sleeves for the first time since landing on Erraid. It was a helter-skelter road, I remember thinking. At one vantage point with a tiny 'v' of Loch Linnhe appearing framed between the hillsides in the distance, it was like looking down a long water staircase until it disappeared into the wood near Coire Ghardail. The road was rough, full of stones and potholes, and I remember offering up a silent prayer – no big blisters at this stage, please. There were occasional glimpses of red deer, skylarks rose straight up into the air singing, and burns murmured out of the hills on both sides. I had lunch beside one of these burns, just beyond Loch Uisge, and my raisins and cheese never tasted better. In that wild place, without distraction, I came to a conclusion: cheese beats dramach any day, unless the dramach is accompanied by sugar or salt or milk or all three.

However, there is a further aberration between RLS's words and the map line on the road to Kingairloch. According to *Kidnapped*, David Balfour made his way with Mr Henderland along the old route, where they met many wayfarers, but the map misses out Kingairloch entirely and strikes Loch Linnhe around Kilmalieu. This route would have involved them in a strenuous march across tough, steep and lonely mountain country and appears to be another slip in detail in the drawing office. David and Mr Henderland chatted as they went on their road, and David learned much about the Disarming Act, priests and Jacobites in hiding, the excruciating poverty of the Stewart tenantry, clan love and loyalty, and the events and principal characters taking centre stage in Appin in the lead-up to the evictions. And as for Allan Breck, said Mr Henderland, 'he's here and awa. He might be glowering at the two of us from yon whin bush, I wouldnae wonder!' As for me, I enjoyed my own company on that most enjoyable hike. I did not set eyes on another soul from the moment I left the main road.

That scene has changed for ever. Part of the road that David Balfour, Mr Henderland and I marched so long ago is now under water. The Loch Uisge basin has recently been turned into a dam and is producing electricity. Of course, a new section of road has been created to retain the link with Lochaline. This was precious, unspoilt wilderness which has arguably been tamed. Yet it is interesting that only a few miles across the hill on the coast one of the biggest holes in the ground in Europe disgorges thousands of tons of rock from the Glensanda stone quarry into waiting ships to be distributed around the world. In Lochaline one of the deepest sand mines in Europe burrows deep into the hillside. Casual visitors pass without even knowing of their existence.

Mr Henderland offered David a bed for the night at his house, standing on its own 'a little beyond Kingairloch'. I had always thought Stevenson intended 'a little beyond Kingairloch' to mean Kilmalieu, which is at least four miles beyond. The more I thought about it, however, the more I began to consider Kilmalieu was too far. Camas na Croise, which means the bay of the cross, is only a mile-and-a-half past Kingairloch, and I began to think this must have been David's stopover. There is also a legend that tells how after James Stewart's body was finally removed from the gallows on top of Cnap a' Chaolais, at Ballachulish, the gibbet was thrown into Loch Linnhe and later washed up on the stony beach at Camas na Croise.

I have discovered no reference to Stevenson travelling in Morvern or Ardgour, and the likelihood is that he did not come this way, but he could have learned of the legend during his research for *Kidnapped* in Appin. However, there is another reason why Stevenson may have had Camas na Croise in mind as the place where David laid his head for the night. In the year *Kidnapped* was published, 1886, the minister at Camas na Croise was a Mr John Henderson – and the name Mr Henderson is but a short step to Mr Henderland, David's walking companion and host. It is possible Stevenson even met Mr Henderson, or that he was at least known to him or his family through their

FIGURE 23. The tiny community of Camas na Croise – the Bay of the Cross – is on the shore of Loch Linnhe. In the centre of the picture is the picturesque Church of Scotland that attracts worshippers from miles around on Sunday afternoons. On the right is the old schoolhouse, which was the manse in Stevenson's time. *Alun John*

Church of Scotland connections. In any event, his name would be listed in the register of ministers. Stevenson took pleasure in using family and friends' names for his characters, and it may be that the Rev. John Henderson was translated into the kindly, snuff-taking catechist Mr Henderland.

Mr Henderson's little house is still standing in Camas na Croise, and long afterwards it became the community school. In the '50s, there was a little boy at that school called Iain Cameron. Iain moved from the area and had a career in social services, and then retired to Dunkeld, but he never forgot his Kingairloch roots. Then a few years ago, the old school house became available to rent and Iain came home to live in the house where he went to school. The teacher's desk and high stool still stand in a corner. Memories of childhood, school pals, the games they played and the fun they had are vivid and everywhere. It falls to few of us to live retrospectively such a happy time in such

PLATE I. The view from Signal Rock in Glencoe looking up the road leading into Gleann Leac na Muidhe. This is possibly one of the escape routes Stevenson had in mind for David Balfour and Allan Breck. They would jump the foaming river below, then clamber up Signal Rock to hide from the searching redcoat soldiers. However, Stevenson does not specify the exact location of these adventures and there are a number of false clues that lead to confusion.

PLATE 2. The old lighthouse keepers' cottages on Erraid looking over the rocky Mull landscape to Ben More in the distance. The cottages have stood the test of time and Erraid's weather for more than a century. *Alun John*

PLATE 3. Round-up time on Erraid with help from John Cameron, who farms Knockvoligan, opposite the islet. As a child John lived on Erraid in the Stevenson house near the pier. Sheep have to make a sea journey to get to market on the mainland. *Alun John*

PLATE 4. Evening at Carsaig with a rain squall on the hills of Jura in the distance. If David Balfour came this way, making for Loch Buie, a rope might have been handy to negotiate the sea cliffs. David's wandering route on Mull is far from clear, but Loch Buie was on one of the sections of the old Pilgrim's Way, which made it a possibility.

PLATE 5. The panorama from Kiel Church at Lochaline looking over the Sound of Mull and the silhouette of Ardtornish Point to the Argyll hills in the background. It must rate among the finest views from a church in Scotland. On the right of the picture the modern-day Torosay ferry approaches Lochaline from Fishnish on Mull.

PLATE 6. Morning reflections at Ballachulish looking towards Glencoe. *Alun John*

PLATE 7. It was through this Glencoe landscape of rock and deep-cut valleys that David and Allan made their escape. Stevenson loved mountains and knew Glencoe well enough to name the old sheep fold of Meannarclach, close to where this picture was taken. Allan Breck had taken a wrong turning in the night, and this was one of the fugitives' possible exit routes. However, their exact Glencoe crossing point remains unclear.

PLATE 8. The Heugh of Coire na Ciche ... this is where Allan Breck came to hide after the murder, and it was in this burn that David and Allan guddled trout. In real life, money for Allan Breck's escape was brought here, along with his French clothes.

PLATE 9. Sgorr na Ciche, or the 'Pap of Glencoe', as it is known, high above
Glencoe village. David Balfour and Allan Breck made their way from the
Aonach Eagach ridge on the right to a point near the summit, before dropping
down to a safe hiding-place in the Heugh of Coire na Ciche above
Caolasnacoan farm on the other side.

PLATE 10. Allan Breck's calling card ... he fashioned a cross and bound to it his silver button, along with sprigs of birch and fir, and placed it in the window of John Breck Maccoll, the bouman at Caolasnacoan. It was a kind of crosstarrie and would have looked similar to this cross placed in the window of the modern-day Caolasnacoan farm. It was Allan Breck's call for help.

PLATE II. The vastness of Rannoch Moor looking towards Schiehallion in the distance on a bright day. In bad weather the Moor can show its teeth even to experienced walkers. It was across this desert that David and Allan made their escape towards Ben Alder out of sight on the left.

PLATE 12. As they emerged from one mass of mountains, a new range with Ben More at its head faced them across the head of Glen Dochart. David's heart must have sunk at the sight. From the Stevenson map the route appears to pass Ben More and Stob Binnein on the west side, but again it becomes confusing here and Stevenson may have played tricks with the landscape.

PLATE 13. David Balfour weather at Rannoch with the white horses on the loch prancing. This is where David and Allan were put across Loch Rannoch making for the high ground above Glen Lyon. While Allan Breck was on the run he stayed with an uncle at Ardlarach within a short distance of the redcoat barracks at Bridge of Gaur.

PLATE 14. Escape from Gullane Sands ... in *Catriona*, the sequel to *Kidnapped*, Allan and David have a last frantic march together to the beach opposite the island of Fidra (above) where the *Thistle* was waiting to spirit Allan Breck to France. It would be near this point that they emerged from the bents, where Allan waded into the sea, leaving David alone on the beach. David was quickly taken prisoner and held on the Bass Rock (below) to prevent him from giving evidence at James Stewart's trial. Stevenson's cousins, the farming Dale family, lived nearby, and therefore this part of the coast was well known to him.

an unusual way – and be reminded of how full and satisfying life could be in such remote communities. Like many youngsters, Iain feels privileged to have gone to school in such a setting, with such people, and that his Kingairloch background has stood him in good stead all his days. And it is certainly not everyone who can say they live in the house where David Balfour had bed-and-breakfast.

Iain's wife Ann has written two valuable historical booklets about Kingairloch church and school, pulling together the threads of their past. On the face of it, Camas na Croise is just a picture postcard church and five houses in a magnificently wild setting, but on Sundays parishioners come from far and near to worship there as they have done for almost 150 years. I joined them one winter's afternoon at 3.30pm, with the light fading. The Rev James Carmichael took the

FIGURE 24. Was this David Balfour's bed-and-breakfast accommodation near Kingairloch? On his travels, David stayed the night at the home of Mr Henderland, the snuff-taking catechist, at a house 'a little beyond Kingairloch'. The old manse at Camas na Croise, occupied by the Rev. Henderson in 1886, the year *Kidnapped* was published, may have been in Stevenson's mind. Mr Henderland organised a boat for David to take him across Loch Linnhe to Appin the following day. *Alun John*

service, as he has done for the last quarter-century or so. He is a busy man with the needs of two other churches at Ardgour and Strontian to tend as well. There was a big turn-out of folk of all ages, including youngsters and even babies. And there was a good feeling about the place. People greeted each other with pleasure and came up to me, as a stranger, and made me feel at home. And Bill Davidson, the church caretaker, a retired estate worker, who once in his enthusiasm almost crowned himself with the church bell as he tolled it, made sure everything was just right. And we all sang lustily while Ann McKinnis from Ardgour struck up on the organ. Mr Carmichael read from the Book of Peter and his sermon struck just the right words and tone. And afterwards we trooped along to the old school house in the dark, David Balfour's resting place and the Camerons' home, and there was tea with goodies all set out as usual, and we did them justice. And we talked about the old days, and the present day, and problems both local and international, and there was a young couple from Lusaka who said their visit to Kingairloch was an experience they would never forget.

I stepped out into the darkness. The lights of Appin glittered from the void across Loch Linnhe. The mountains looked down and I stopped to listen to the water and the sounds of the night. A movement against the lighter background of one of the houses caught my eye. I could just make out the shape and hatstand antlers of a red deer stag. He was browsing on the grass beside the church. Then I remembered, of course, he was either Glen or Grouch, the stags I had been told about that had become partly tame. To the passer-by I suppose Kingairloch doesn't seem much. But for those who live there, or are in the know, it is the worth of the folk behind those doors that really counts, and I found myself in total agreement with the sentiments of the couple from Lusaka.

All those years ago, when I first marched in David's footsteps, I mistakenly thought Camas na Croise was Kingairloch. In fact, Kingairloch is out of sight, below the road at the head of Loch a' Choire, inevitably nowadays with a salmon farm in its jaws. It is a peaceful, serene scene down there behind the trees, hills on three sides and in a little out-of-sight world of its own, with Kingairloch House at the far end of the loch. I have now enjoyed many a happy wander there.

David Balfour hitched a lift on a boat in this area over to Appin. I had hoped to do likewise but I gave myself little chance. I reasoned, however, that there might be people about in the morning and I could at least ask. My feet were troubling me after the hard roads, so I soaked them in a burn, while I ate my evening meal. I decided to end my day on a note of luxury. Rather than another round of dramach, I boiled water for creative porridge for dinner. That meant making real porridge and bunging in a handful of raisins. Porridge purists might not be too appreciative, but in the absence of milk, porridge broth or stew is not to be decried in the right circumstances and setting.

I dropped down into the wood above Kingairloch House, but below the road and settled in for the night. I could see the stars above the trees. This is the life, I thought, and remembered Stevenson's lines from 'The Vagabond':

> Bed in the bush with stars to see,
> Bread I dip in the river,
> There's the life for a man like me,
> There's the life for ever.

And another great day, I thought. Great country, great weather, great hike, great feeling. Across the Torosay ferry, fishing with balloons, St Columba, Viking invaders, the agony of the Clearances. And it's not every day you see a fox fight a buzzard.

7

The March to Murder Wood

How David Balfour hitched a lift by boat, but I have to take the long way to the Wood of Lettermore and count my blisters; how I meet a Gaelic-speaking horse, and am attacked by clouds of voracious midges like David before me, and finally find the place where the Red Fox was shot in the back.

David had more luck than I at Kingairloch. Not only did Mr Henderland give him a bed for the night, but next day he found a man with a boat to take him over the Linnhe Loch into Appin. As for me, there was only one thing for it – hoist my pack and steel myself for a long hike. Without a boat the only way to reach the Wood of Lettermore, where Colin Campbell met his end, is by the Corran Ferry at Ardgour. Loch Linnhe narrows here and the ferry links with the busy Fort William-Glencoe road. After that, I could see, it was merely a matter of following the main road to the next ferry at North Ballachulish. From Corran, however, I would be following in the footsteps this time of Colin Campbell of Glenure as he made his fateful way from Fort William to the same crossing-point. The Wood of Lettermore, where David was set down from his boat and where the Red Fox met his violent end, was about half-a-mile beyond the ferry. All told, I estimated it would be a hike of nearly 30 miles. The Wood of Lettermore was therefore my target for the day.

I was not particularly looking forward to it. My feet were still tender from the previous day, and much of the walking to Appin on this route would be on hard, metalled roads. I knew from experience what mischief that could cause. In the army, when the blisters grew, we used to say 'the dogs were barking'. By the time I reached Lettermore, I thought, 'the dogs' might be howling. The map indicated I would be retracing my footsteps to some extent, but on the other side of the loch, to arrive at the same place as David in his boat. I knew my chances of finding a boat were slim and, as it turned out, I didn't see a soul for the next five miles to ask if anyone might be going my way. Appin and Ardgour stare at each other from across the barrier of Loch Linnhe, but they might as well be in France or Norway for all the contact they have with each other. I could tell from a glance at the map that my detour would take me a full day and I grudged the time lost from my main journey. Anyway, let's get it over with, I thought, and struck up a brisk pace.

I was fortunate with the weather. It was a bright, sunny day with a light breeze and the road runs more or less along the flat above the lochside. Within ten minutes of setting out, my whole mood changed. The air was sparkling, the hills sharp and clear, the sun on the waves threw dazzling light spears all over the loch, and I remembered David had encountered something of the same on his boat crossing. In his case, however, the sun was shining on little moving clumps of red on the Appin shore, and every now and then there came sparks and lightnings as though the sun had struck upon bright steel. David was seeing the redcoat soldiers on the march from Fort William against the poor tenantry, as he put it.

For me it was a delight to go swinging along that road from Kingairloch in such country. The blood was singing in my veins and I felt up for anything. The road twists and turns, bobs and weaves, even seems to somersault once or twice as it momentarily vanishes over unexpected humps. It is some road. For a hiker it is a joy, for a driver it is a keep-your-concentration road, a one-car-wide frolicsome road, with unexpected hazards like red deer, strolling sheep, fluttering hoodie crows and, for me, on one occasion, even two otters happily sunning themselves. In daylight, the distraction for drivers is undoubtedly the Ardgour hills on the left, with their deep-running glens and high tops; and on the right, the shimmering Loch Linnhe with the whole Appin coastline catching your breath on the other side. The best advice to drivers is pull over and give in to the scenery. Count on it being a long journey because you will stop often. It is a little-travelled slice of Scotland to relish.

With the help of the map, I could pick out some of the places I wanted to visit on the distant shore. There was Shuna Island, and I

FIGURE 25. The Appin coastline across Loch Linnhe from Ardgour. In the centre is the distinctive nose of Sgorr na Ciche at the end of the Aonach Eagach above Glencoe. The dark headland to its right is where David Balfour was set ashore in Appin Murder country.

knew dramatic Castle Stalker, traditional stronghold of the Stewarts, was just behind it off Portnacroish. As I progressed further, I could see Cuil Bay and I knew this was the beginning of *Kidnapped* country. Glen Duror cut into the mountainside above and, at the foot of the glen, out of sight, stood James Stewart's farm of Acharn. Duror gave me my bearings to locate the ruined Keil church, where James's bones were taken from the scaffold and secretly buried. Sure enough, there it was right down by the lochside. Ardshiel House, home of Charles Stewart, Captain of the Appin Regiment, would be in the trees on the high ground this side of Kentallen Bay. With a little thrill I recognised this was the edge of Murder Country.

Ardgour tends to be overlooked by climbers and visitors. Perhaps just as well because it is hard country. The Ardgour hills are not the highest tops, but they rise more or less straight off Loch Linnhe's shoreline and are deceptively rounded from a distance. Up close, they are full of gullies, glens, ridges, scree and cliff faces. Behind Ardgour's enticing appeal lurks mountain treachery for those who think these hills are not to be taken seriously. I once climbed Creach Bheinn and Maol Odhar in winter with a friend. The weather swung from sunshine to mist, then a snow whiteout, and I wished I was elsewhere. Mist distorts everything and we needed the compass as well as the map, while unexpected chasms seemed to yawn up at us out of nowhere. We were glad to get down.

But this was a day of sunshine and cottonwool clouds, people- and traffic-free. I walked on the grass where possible to save my feet. Eventually a van came up behind me, stopped, too, and a chatty driver offered me a lift. He was going to Fort William, he said, taking the scenic route, he added with a chuckle. If I liked he could drop me at Corran. I heard myself say thank you, but no thanks. Even as I said it, I knew I had made a mistake. But I was enjoying the hike and it was all new and exciting country for me. By evening I would have gone on bended knee for a lift.

One of my priorities was to find a shop where I could restock with cheese and raisins. I had enough to get by, but in case of emergency, I wanted to top up. I thought I would also indulge in more chocolate and a quarter of boiled sweets. The chocolate dispenses energy, the boilings comfort. When the going gets tough, pop in a boiling; when sleeping out after a hard day suck on a boiling. Boilings, advised an old climber friend, will bring you a sense of wellbeing. I hoped Corran would be able to supply my needs.

By the time I arrived at the ferry, the 'dogs' were barking, but I had other distractions. Looking over Loch Leven to that sword slash through the mountains called Glencoe is one of Scotland's most unforgettable sights. As I marched along in slow motion against the scale of Appin, I was able to pinpoint the Wood of Lettermore (or the Wood of Ballachulish as it has also been called) and study the murder site terrain and landscape from a distance. Somewhat depressingly, however, it now seemed a very long hike and and my forecast was a limp at the end of it.

The ferry over the narrow crossing at Corran operated much as it does today, although as far as I can remember it ran less frequently and was certainly much cheaper then. As I arrived, it was about to take off, so I jumped aboard. I enjoyed the short trip for two reasons: firstly, from midway there is a conversation-stopping view right up Glen Albyn and Glen Mor, by Loch Lochy towards Loch Ness, straight as a pole along the line of the Caledonian Canal; and on the other side, the panorama stretches right down the widening Loch Linnhe to the island of Lismore and towards Mull and the out-of-sight Oban. I have since made this crossing many times, but none surpassed that day of sunshine, calm and reflections on that Loch Linnhe mirror. My other interest was the little lighthouse above the slipway on the Ardgour shore. Yes, it, too, was Stevenson-built.

As I came to the main road and turned right for the Ballachulish ferry, I knew I was then following the route Colin Campbell of Glenure had taken on the day of his murder. He had been in Fort William, or Maryburgh, as it was still sometimes known, with his lawyer nephew from Edinburgh, Mungo Campbell, and his servant John Mackenzie. Donald Kennedy, the sheriff-officer from Inveraray, had come up to join them on May 13, bringing the warrant for 'ejecting certain possessors of the lands of Ardshiel'. Kennedy's role was to be employed in 'executing the ejection'. The following morning, they set off from Fort William on their mission. It was to be carried out on May 15. The countdown to Glenure's murder was underway. He had booked ahead in Kentallen Inn for the night. The landlord there was also facing eviction, which gives an indication of the changes in ownership and custom taking place in Appin still in the aftermath of Culloden. Kennedy was on foot and set off early; the others took the horse-road, which connected with what was known then as the King's Road, heading for the Ballachulish ferry. It says much for Glenure's courage as he left the Fort on his last journey that he gave no sign of apprehension, although he knew he could be shot from a bush at any moment.

What they did not meet, however, was a large white van parked in a layby, with the driver outside on a chair taking his ease, munching his 'piece', sipping tea from a china cup, and reading the *Daily Record*. It was my lucky day. This was just the chap I wanted to meet. Cars were still few and far between then, and many country areas, as well as towns, relied on their delivery van for necessities. Whoever designed and packed these mobile shops thought of everything. From bread to firelighters, custard to paraffin, milk to turnips, tapioca to Zebo, hair-pins to writing paper, the vans would have them stowed away in their right place. The van driver was friend to everyone, and also a main line of communication, carrying messages, even parcels, between remote neighbours, while keeping a watchful eye on their health and interests. Finding my cheese, raisins, chocolate and boilings was a matter of moments. He suggested some bananas, and I bought them, too. I asked if he had any sticking plaster to add to my supply. Big ones, please, for big blisters, and he sympathetically produced the biggest ones I had ever seen. Take care of the 'dogs', he advised, and they will take care of you. I shared a cuppa with him, the driver on his chair, me sitting on his van step. As a parting gift, he handed me a meat pie. I could have had no greater gesture of friendship.

But there was no escape for the 'dogs' on that hard road. I could feel the blisters growing. My feet were certainly hotter, they also felt bigger and heavier. Whenever I stopped for a rest, I began to look for places where I could sit down and raise them high. The relief was unbelievable. The higher the feet, the better and faster the recovery. Fences, I found, were perfect for this joy. I could lie on my back and simply drape my boots over a wire. The relief was instant. I decided to aim for a suitable fence every mile. By the time I had reached Ballachulish I was looking for a fence every half-mile, counting the telegraph poles and limping badly.

When Glenure reached Ballachulish ferry, he was late. Donald Kennedy, even on foot, was waiting for him. In those days the ferry did not run between the Loch Leven narrows like its motorised successor, where the road bridge now stands. The currents were too strong and it was a journey frequently needing both sail and oars. Glenure's ferry left the Callart side between Onich and North Ballachulish, and the pier on the south side was midway between the Ballachulish Hotel of today and Lettermore. There were two ferrymen then, one on each shore, employed by the tenants, who shared the fares. It was an arrangement Glenure also wanted to end.

My journey was also slow. Not only was my pace in bottom gear, but I had stopped for half-an-hour to examine the murder location in detail from the other side of the loch. This is the grandstand seat for a perspective of all the key sites, the contours of the hillside, the distances, the escape routes, the line of the old road. Figures can also be seen, but at too great a distance for recognition. It meant, of course, that the assassin could also have seen his quarry approaching on the Onich side. If unable to identify Glenure, he would at least be alerted that riders were on their way. There was no secret about Glenure's

FIGURE 26. Mist trails off Beinn a' Bheithir above Loch Linnhe. It was near
this spot on the lochside that Colin Campbell was taken by ferry to the far
shore on the way to his death. The murder took place above the shoreline in
the Wood of Lettermore on the extreme right of the picture. The assassin's
escape route was most likely in the wooded ground on the right. At night, after
the murder, Allan Breck made his way along the loch to the left towards
Glencoe and Caolasnacoan.

movements and the whole area knew he intended to stay overnight in
Kentallen. There was no other route he could take.

I crossed on the ferry in the company of two cars, a van and one of
the travelling folk with a horse and small cart. The horse was not happy.
It had made this journey before and did not like the sensation of sailing
or the vibration of the engine. One of the crew spoke to it kindly, then
tried to lead it on by the bridle. Its owner stood at the rear grinning, and
steadying his load of logs, which had a small boy perched on top. The
horse was not for moving. It was leaning backwards, its forelegs in tug-
o'-war stance. The travelling man then took command. He said with an
even bigger grin: 'Nae yis speakin' tae Rory in English for he only kens
Gaelic'. At this he roared with lilting laughter, and we all laughed with
him. He gave Rory a pat, a sniff of his woodsmoke jacket, and conversed
gently with the horse unmistakably in the 'language of the Garden of
Eden', as one of my Gael friends used to call it. With that he gave a

couple of clicks of his tongue in that international horse language that means 'go', and Rory trotted happily aboard. To this day I don't know if Rory really was a Gaelic-speaking horse or if the travelling man was having a private joke at our expense.

The ferry deposited us on the slipway outside the Ballachulish Hotel, a comfortable Appin tryst for many years. The iron bridge across the narrows was not built until 1976, but the car ferry, when I crossed, was fast, efficient and cheap and handled the volume of vehicles with ease. I came across an old price card for the ferry dated 1932 when sheep cost a penny each to cross, stirks 6d, cows a shilling and a horse and cart 3s 6d. These prices were considered exorbitant at the time. It is a measure of the spread of the motor car over 40 years that today the ferry would be a joke. At the height of summer, the bridge traffic becomes a two-way thundering herd with three-way destinations – over to Fort William, Ben Nevis, the West Highlands and on to Inverness; up to Glencoe, the massacre site, the mountains and the South; or down to Oban, its ferries and the Hebrides beyond. Once on the way, it is difficult to stop when traffic is heavy; the compulsion is to keep driving, and many visitors might as well be in aeroplanes, skimming over Scotland, never knowing and hardly seeing it.

Now I really was in *Kidnapped* country. Directly above my head was Cnap a' Chaolais, where James Stewart was strung up on the gibbet. Although I couldn't see the cairn marking the place, I knew it would take only a couple of minutes to climb up to it. The truth is I couldn't face the climb. I was really beginning to suffer. All I wanted to do was take the weight off my aching feet and settle down in some comfortable, mossy wood. Here was I on the doorstep of the Appin Murder, something I had been planning for years, and my feet were too sore to concentrate. Terrible! I'll be back tomorrow, I said to myself, or at least the next day, and I limped on my way along the Oban road towards the Wood of Lettermore, the 'dogs' whimpering with every step.

As I left the ferry slipway, I could see Lettermore about a mile ahead. In slow motion I shambled towards it. But the excitement of being at the hub of Appin Murder country, and all the events I had read about, and Stevenson and *Kidnapped*, and the mystery and the murder hunt, made me think in exclamation marks. I had the map out to identify everything.

Look at the mountains! Unbelievable! There's the Pap of Glencoe! That's where Allan Breck hid, in the heugh of Coire na Ciche. There's Ballachulish House! That's where they found the gun in the yew tree! Look, there's the burn! That's where Allan Breck went fishing on the day of the murder! I dragged my throbbing feet a little farther and, yes, there's the old ferry pier where Glenure and his party landed! Now I was stepping in the footsteps of Colin Campbell of Glenure minutes before that fatal shot.

I came to a point where, I guessed, Glenure had dismounted and walked with the Ballachulish laird. Was he in on the killing, I wondered. The lie of the land gave me an indication where the old road must have left the lochside to climb into the wood. A few limps farther and I came to the place where I judged David Balfour, with the help of his boat, must have arrived in Appin fresh and ready for adventure. I was arriving dead beat and ready for sleep. I had noticed a large rock sticking into the water as I hobbled along the lochside beside the old Oban-Ballachulish 'Gaelic Express' railway line. The rock was big enough for several men to stand upon and I had made up my mind that to reach it would definitely be my last steps for the day.

The tide was well in, I tottered across the rails and half fell down the bank to get to the water's edge. I had one thing only in my thoughts – get the boots off and the 'dogs' into Loch Linnhe.

Indeed my feet were in poor shape. Blisters big and small everywhere. I was surprised Loch Linnhe didn't bubble as my feet entered the water. The sheer luxury of not walking was excelled only by the sheer ecstasy of the cold wavelets caressing my blisters. I lay there for ten minutes luxuriating, a silly smile on my face, my eyes shut. I was in Heaven.

Unfortunately, my troubles were not quite over. The feet continued in paradise for a few seconds longer, but suddenly the rest of me came under vicious assault from that scourge of Scotland – the Great Highland Midge and his band of man-eaters in full cry. Battalions of them, dancing in the air with joy, swooping in on attack after attack. Get away from the water. Fast. Only solution. Move now. I crammed my blisters into my boots sockless. Forget laces. Run for it. Bitter experience was speaking. I scrambled up the bank, over the railway track and back onto the road. Alacrity is what comes into play to escape from raging tigers. I was alacrity personified.

I once took a group of Robert Louis Stevenson Club members over the same ground in early May. The words 'We're lucky at this time of year because it is too early for the Great Highland Midge' had just passed my lips when I noticed a terrible fidgeting, scratching of ears and noses, and rubbing of eyes, among the dignified members, followed by much swiping of the air. Clearly the voracious Appin midge did not know the rules. Even David Balfour, as he stood at the same spot, referred to 'being troubled by a cloud of stinging midges'. Had midges been peckish around 5.30pm on May 14, 1752, the Appin assassin could well have missed his shot.

It was then both 'dogs', at last, began to howl. Poor things, they had finally had enough. Messed about and deceived into thinking their agony was over, they took their revenge. So what to do now? I remembered from the map that a path should take me up into the Wood of Lettermore. Sweet sleep on a murder site was suddenly appealing. With my bare feet flapping in my boots, I hobbled up the track as if it were strewn with white-hot sharpened nails.

And then I saw it, a small, inconspicuous pile of stones bound by mortar. I hirpled down and read the plaque. It said simply without comment: 'This cairn is erected on the spot where Colin Campbell of Glenure was murdered' and gave the date.

I tried to picture the scene as it was described by Stevenson. David Balfour had been sitting in the wood full of self-doubt about his next step when there came a sound of men and horses. Presently, after a turning in the road, he saw four travellers come into view. The first was a great, red-headed gentleman, with an imperious and flushed face, who carried his hat in his hand and fanned himself:

"Can ye tell me the way to Aucharn", David had suddenly stood up and asked the big red-headed man.

"And what seek ye in Aucharn?" said Colin Campbell; him they call the Red Fox; for he it was I had stopped.

"The man that lives there," said I.

"James of the Glens", says Glenure musingly; and then to the lawyer: "Is he gathering his people, think ye?"

But just as he turned there came the shot of a firelock from higher up the hill; and with the very sound of it Glenure fell upon the road. "Oh, I am dead!", he cried several times over.

This was the shot that killed Glenure, that led to the hanging of James of the Glen (not 'Glens' as Stevenson had it), created the mystery of the 'unknown' assassin and so fascinated Stevenson that he wrote *Kidnapped*. This was the precise spot – but all I could think about were my feet.

Coming up the hill, I discovered by walking on my toes my right foot was a fraction less painful and, when I walked on my heels, the left foot, too, seemed less excruciating. So I did a kind of hornpipe on tiptoe into the trees searching for a suitable place to lay me down with a will. I spread my groundsheet, the boots were off in a blink, I snowed baby powder like a blizzard on to the blisters, and pulled on clean socks. The blisters will receive full attention in the morning, I decided with a yawn. Without leaving my groundsheet square, I pulled out my sleeping bag and arranged myself, with the help of the contours of the ground and my rucksack, into a kind of boomerang shape, with my head higher than my stomach, but my feet higher than my head. I ate a fistful of raisins, a banana and took a gulp of water.

FIGURE 27. The view from the Ballachulish bridge a few strides from where James Stewart was hanged. In the background are the Ardgour hills with Kingairloch out of sight on the left. The wooded promontory in the centre is where David Balfour landed and Colin Campbell was shot.

Tea could also wait till morning. It was a warm spring evening with a clear sky. I hardly needed the sleeping bag, but I struggled into it and lay in repose with my hands behind my head. Bliss! Sore feet, sure, but a great day just the same, I thought. And here I am in Appin.

My eyes had still to close when I heard that familiar high-pitched buzz and a sharp pinprick on my nose. Midges! I reached down into the bottom of my rucksack and found what I was looking for. It was my woolly balaclava, normally worn only on mountain tops in extreme ice and snow conditions. Had I brought gloves, I would have donned them, too. I pulled my balaclava down over my ears until only my eyes were visible. I popped two boilings into my mouth, pulled the sleeping bag over my head, wiped away a bead of perspiration, and prepared to simmer the night away. Anything was better than facing those little devils.

8

A Detective Joins the Case

How Colin Campbell of Glenure was shot in the back
from a concealed position in the Wood of Lettermore,
and I find suspects abound; Allan Breck goes fishing, and
I cast some new light on the crime with the help of a
Campbell, the Argyll and Sutherland Highlanders and a
detective.

When I first visited the spot where Colin Campbell was shot in the
Wood of Lettermore, the surrounding terrain was unspoiled. The
present fir wood had not been planted 40 years ago and Lettermore
and the hillside above would have been virtually as they were on the
afternoon of the shooting.

It is unfortunate an area containing an important historical site
should have been so disturbed and distorted by the Forestry
Commission. On that first visit, the section of the old road along
which Glenure travelled on the day of his murder was clearly visible.
It was overgrown through lack of use, but its uphill course was still
discernible, and could even be followed in parts. It was more
track than road, and protruding rocks, stones and roots made it
obviously treacherous for horses. Near where the murder took place
the slope of the road began to flatten, following the contour of the
hillside, although that flank of the hill itself was very steep. The
planting and felling of the trees have ensured the original road has
been lost for ever.

The area where the murderer hid while waiting for Glenure has also
been disturbed. After 250 years the Forestry Commission perhaps
considered the matter of little interest. They were wrong. The site has
always drawn many people to examine and ponder the event that took
place there and controversially cost a man his life on the gallows.

Historians, film makers, politicians, clansmen, writers – including Robert Louis Stevenson – have all visited it.

The Forestry Commission's decision to plant across the site must have been debated at the time. The easy option was to leave a little more respectful space around the cairn and its immediate vicinity. Someone somewhere thought it wasn't worth bothering about. This decision was insensitive and showed little acknowledgement or understanding of a piece of Scottish history. It is true that in recent times the Forestry Commission has tried to make amends by taking down trees and improving access, but the damage is irrecoverable.

When I first stood at the cairn it was on a mid-May day. I always pictured the murderer lifting his musket, lining up the sights on Glenure's back and taking a long shot from high on the hillside. Now at the scene I was immediately struck by the short distances involved. For a start, a long-range shot was not necessary. A flank of the hill only 50 feet or so above the path gave perfect cover for a sniper and also offered a fast escape route. The hillside, too, at this point was much steeper than I had thought. A long shot would have been a difficult one. Glenure would have been at a sharp angle below the marksman and from high ground could have presented a tricky and mostly left-sided target. This marksman didn't want to take chances. He couldn't afford to be seen because that might cause panic and sharp movement and make the target more difficult to hit. This sniper wanted to be sure. He did not want Glenure wounded. He wanted him dead.

The ambush site where the murderer hid must surely, I reckoned, be much lower on the hillside. The assassin wouldn't want to be hurried. He would want to choose his spot carefully. He would want to see without being seen, have a clear view and make it a simple, telling shot. The position was chosen because the road was rough and the horses would be forced to take their time. A slow-moving target was the best. The gunman would not know whether Glenure would be in the saddle or dismounted to lead his horse over the uneven ground. It was possible the horse could get between the assassin and Glenure and that could make the target chancy. Well, there were always risks.

There would be no squeamishness whether the shot was in Glenure's back, front, head or heart. It was the right shot at the right place and time that mattered. Every step had to be considered to ensure it did its job. All this would be in the mind of the man who pulled the trigger. The murder of Colin Campbell was the work of a trained professional. This is not surprising because there were plenty of veteran soldiers around from the 'Forty-Five campaign with no affection for Campbells, and who would be prepared to take the shot or advise a younger man on how it should be done. Poor Glenure at the time was the most reviled man in the area.

The other factors in the gunman's favour were that he had plenty of time in advance to select and try out his best position. He could be out of sight quickly after the shot was fired and it would be difficult to track his movements. The element of surprise was his. The sounds of the muskets of the day were like a cannon's roar, accompanied by a mighty puff of smoke, but he wouldn't have been worried about the shot attracting attention. In spite of the fact that all weapons were prohibited, gunshots were commonplace and there was no shortage of guns in the area. In fact, in their evidence at the trial of James Stewart, both Donald Kennedy and John Mackenzie noted the shot that killed Glenure yet attached no importance to it until they heard Mungo Campbell wailing. Apart from Glenure, game for the pot was the most likely target in Appin at the time.

When I visited the scene in 1960, I tried to put myself in the murderer's place. I scouted the hillside looking for what was likely to be the best position for an assassination attempt. From the high ground, it would indeed have been a difficult downhill shot, and the Wood of Lettermore at the time of the murder was described as being thick and full of bushes. The chances were, I considered, that the gunman might have been forced into taking a standing shot. That was undesirable because, firstly, the hitman could be seen; secondly, it increased the possibility of wounding Glenure or missing him entirely. The guns used in those days were long and heavy, and for a shot from up the hill the assassin would have felt happier, I guessed, with something to lean on to steady the barrel. The assassin's slightest movement might have been seen from below, in which case Glenure and his party could quickly have taken evasive action. A fast-moving target aimed at from high on the hill would be the last thing the gunman wanted.

No, the shot surely had to come from much lower down. I tried to remember my infantry training. Again I began to scour the hillside.

FIGURES 28 AND 29. Above: Take aim, steady, squeeze ... this is the assassin's view from his concealed position in the Wood of Lettermore. Members of the Robert Louis Stevenson Club stand beside the cairn marking the place where Glenure died. Below: The author indicates where the murderer lay hidden near the bush in the background.

The spring grasses and bracken by May at Lettermore are well up and that particular side of the hill is full of bumps, depressions, bulges, tussocks of grass and rock. In the right position, they could easily conceal a prone figure. I began to look at these more closely. I want to be certain I don't miss, I said to myself, so I want to be as near my target as possible. I don't want to stand and I don't want to be seen. What would be the ideal position?

If possible, I want to be almost level with my target to give me the easiest shot, but that isn't going to be practicable. To hit Glenure in the back, the shot must have been fired almost directly from behind, but perhaps not as high as I had at first thought. I'd choose as low a point as I dared to be sure of making the shot count. I began to examine the ground behind the cairn. Ideally, again, I would want to take the shot from a lying position, with the barrel supported perhaps by a rest or even the ground in front. I began to walk up and down the hillside at different levels and different distances from the cairn looking at different angles. Of course, all this is academic if the murder cairn is in the wrong place, I pondered, but I have no reason to believe that it is.

Trying to make this positional logic work, with a little tingle of excitement I came upon a depression that was tailor-made for the task. It was just the size of a man lying down. Let's say the cairn is Glenure, I said to myself, what kind of a shot is he going to make from here? I lay down in the cavity and squinted along a handy piece of stick. The new grass and fern provided full cover. I simply vanished. Perfect! Mounted on his horse, Glenure's back would be big and broad and high. He would be looking ahead or concentrating on the rough trail below his horse's hooves. Glenure was a sitting duck.

The assassin could have lain low, face down, gun stretched in front of him and lined up at the road only slightly below. An army could have passed and been unaware of his presence. All the unknown assassin had to do was wait until Glenure had passed, then lift his head, maybe even take time to part the grass, take aim – and bang! He could have gently stood up or knelt on one knee before firing. It was the easiest hit a sniper ever made. The way Glenure's party was spread out along the narrow path was fortuitous, but even if they had all been clustered around him, at that distance the result was likely to have been the same.

I felt very satisfied. But, of course, I couldn't be sure it was the exact spot from where the assassin squeezed the trigger. The ground was virtually as it was in 1752, it was the same month and also the same time of around 5.30pm. If it was not the precise spot where the assassin lay in wait, then I felt confident it was very close.

Shortly after this discovery, I learned of a young Argyll and Sutherland Highlander officer who was using the Appin Murder as a training exercise for his soldiers. He had read up on the various suspects in the case, as well as those who gave evidence at the subsequent trial. His soldiers were examining the movements of some of these witnesses, timing them, testing their statements on the ground and generally doing some of the detective work that should have been undertaken 208 years earlier. What a good idea, I thought! It seemed to me that Lieutenant Alastair Campbell of Airds could be casting some interesting new light on that very old murder mystery.

The name Campbell of Airds also caught my attention. Surely it was Campbell of Airds who was the friend of James Stewart of the Glen. He had kindly offered James the renting of Acharn farm when eviction loomed at Achindarroch. It was Campbell of Airds who had been prevented from giving evidence on James's behalf at the trial. I felt it was imperative that this present-day Campbell of Airds and I met to discuss our mutual interest.

This young Campbell of Airds indeed turned out to be the great-great-great-great grandson of James Stewart's friend. We made our arrangements and I found Alastair and some of his Argylls at the murder spot waiting for me. Alastair was tall and lanky, in battledress top and kilt, and sporting a natty pair of wellies. He and his soldiers had driven up from Stirling Castle that morning. We compared notes and theories, walked and scrambled over the ground, studying it in detail, and slowly began to reconstruct the murder using different scenarios. What was immediately interesting was the fact that, acting separately, Alastair had already deduced that the point from where the assassin struck was the same depression on the hillside that I had found.

What I appreciated about Alastair's approach was that it was matter-of-fact, painstaking and practical. He was not for snatching at superficial conclusions. He wanted everything based, tried and tested on known fact. His Argylls loved the exercise. They threw themselves into it with gusto. The debriefing went on into the early hours of the morning.

Alastair and his men did not come up with major revelations, but one important finding was established. It is entirely possible to move from the vicinity of Ballachulish House to the murder cairn and back without being seen. In police parlance, it brought one of the key suspects, who had been excluded, back into the frame.

The years have rolled on since that exercise was completed. The landscape then was in its pristine pre-Forestry Commission shape. Now the mature trees are being taken down and 'the scene of crime' has been 'contaminated' for ever. After completing his career in the Argylls, with some adventures in Nigeria, and later becoming managing director of Waverley Vintners, Alastair Campbell is now the

FIGURES 30 AND 31. In 1960 Alastair Campbell of Airds (left) was a young lieutenant in the Argyll and Sutherland Highlanders trying to cast new light on the Appin Murder with the help of a platoon of his Argylls on a training exercise. Separately, Ian Nimmo was trying to do the same thing. They linked up at the time to compare notes at the murder scene. Alastair is the great-great-great-great grandson of the Campbell of Airds who was friend to James Stewart of the Glen. Forty years later, Alastair and the author met again at the same spot for a BBC Radio Scotland programme to mark the 250th anniversary of Colin Campbell's death.

distinguished and much-respected Clan Campbell historian and author of one of the most detailed clan histories ever written. We were delighted to link up again at the same scene after all those years in 2002, during the making of a BBC Radio Scotland series to mark the 250th anniversary of the murder. Alastair, whose shadow has expanded somewhat since I knew him first as that slim, dashing young lieutenant (but then my hair in the interim has gone with the wind), has not altered his views on the murder, the trial or verdict. He still believes on the weight of evidence that Allan Breck was involved in the shooting and James Stewart properly hanged because he was an accomplice. On the other hand, nothing has altered my own view: I still believe James was innocent and the lack of evidence against Allan Breck makes his case not proven.

More years passed, and with fly rods swishing, I was sharing a boat on Cobbinshaw Loch in West Lothian with the late Malcolm Thomson, Scottish international angler, but perhaps more importantly, a former head of Edinburgh, Lothians and Borders CID. Murder was Malcolm's business, past and present, so I tried him with the Appin Murder. How do you solve a 250-year-old murder, I asked him. He was at once fascinated. I was surprised he knew so much about it, but his knowledge was largely based on several readings of *Kidnapped*, which had caught his imagination in boyhood. 'Why don't you bring some modern police methodology to bear on the case?' suggested Malcolm. 'Even today, you may be surprised what it turns up.'

So I contacted my old school friend, retired Detective Inspector Les Liney from Pitlochry, a trusted, experienced hand who had also handled a few murder cases in his day. The idea of investigating an ancient murder with such a cold trail caught Les's fancy. He began to read up on what detail was available and I fed him everything I knew.

First off, had it happened today, suggested DI Liney, an independent police force would have been brought in to take over the inquiry. At the time, the Campbells were more or less in charge of the whole investigation. They represented law and order by government decree, but simultaneously the Campbells, in this case, were driven by personal revenge and conditioned by centuries of clan malice. In particular, John Campbell, Glenure's half-brother, laird of the adjoining estate of Barcaldine, was virtually in command.

It was at the instigation of John Campbell that James was arrested; it was John Campbell who, without warrant, had James's home searched and evidence that may have worked in his favour removed; it was John Campbell who ensured James was kept in solitary confinement in Fort William without access to legal advice. Under Scots law the accused is taken into the protection of the court to ensure he or she receives a fair trial. In the case of James Stewart, he was taken into custody to ensure he hanged. John Campbell helped to select the 11 Campbell jurors for James's trial, and although Campbell of Stonefield was Sheriff of Argyll, and Colonel John Crawford was commander of the Fort William garrison, and others were carrying out the orders, it was John Campbell of Barcaldine who was making all the running.

With another police force in place, said Les Liney, the next step would be to identify everyone who might have heard or seen anything that could cast light on what actually happened. On one side, the Stewarts and their friends would close ranks and give away as little as possible to avoid incriminating one of their own. At a superficial first glance, the murder had all the hallmarks of a community conspiracy, but the important point would be to keep an open mind to allow the jigsaw to be built up by legwork and asking the right questions of the right people. On the Campbells' side – which was also the government's side – it had to be appreciated that witnesses would be largely hostile towards James or anything that savoured of Jacobitism. Centuries of clan hatred would colour every statement.

In these circumstances, the only course of action by an independent police force would be hard individual questioning. If need be, a little leaning might take place on those who had something to give or hide.

Forensic science, like matching gun to bullets, finger printing or DNA, was unknown then, but a *post mortem* report provided valuable evidence. After the shooting, Colin Campbell's body was carried to the big rock that sticks into Loch Linnhe just below the place where the murder was committed. From there it was taken by boat to Kentallen and eventually home to Glenure farm. The following day, two surgeons carried out separate examinations there.

The more detailed examination was carried out by Patrick Campbell of Achnaba. It indicated that two bullets had entered Glenure's body at the back, one on either side of the spine, and exited through his abdomen. On its passage, one of the bullets pierced the liver. The points where the bullets struck Glenure were two-and-a-half inches apart. One of the bullets came out just below his navel and the other about 'six or seven inches' from it towards the right side, possibly having been deflected by spinal tissue. While Achnaba undertook a proper *post mortem* examination, the other surgeon involved, Alexander Campbell, made a less detailed study of the body. One bullet emerged about an inch below the navel, he stated, and the other two inches from it. Strangely, it was Alexander Campbell's less comprehensive report that was presented at James's trial.

The question of one shot and two wounds in Glenure's body is not a mystery. It was the practice then to load two lead bullets into the same gun, one half the size of the other. The second, smaller and less accurate, bullet was called the *ruagaire*, the chaser, or the *fear siubhail*, the wanderer, because it wavered in flight. In fact, the two wounds tended to confirm only one shot had been fired. Had two shots been fired and hit their target, then four wounds would have been expected.

These autopsy reports were of great interest to my detective friend. It was Les Liney's belief that they indicated the shot had been fired at very close range. The fact that both entry points were so close, and the force of both bullets took them entirely through Glenure's body, suggested a very short distance was involved. If the shot had been fired from higher up the hill, as most people have believed, the spread would have been wider and the bullets, or at least one of them, would more likely have remained lodged in the body. The trajectory in relation to the positioning of the entry and exiting bullet holes also gave an indication, said Les, that they were fired from much lower on the hillside than had previously been considered.

But where on that hillside did the assassin hide? The trajectory gave us a clue. We began to examine the ground in detail just as I had done 40 years previously. Not that we were going to find anything new or produce a revelation, but somehow it seemed important just to pinpoint where the murderer lay in wait so that we could better picture the scene. Eventually, Les stopped: 'My guess is that he would be about here,' he said. 'He had to be within a couple of yards of where I'm standing.' It was exactly the spot, as far as I could see after the disturbance to the ground, where Alastair Campbell and I had separately found that man-size depression so perfectly tailored for a sniper.

It was precisely 21 yards behind the cairn and at a shallow angle. We also measured how long it would have taken for the murderer to pull the trigger, then disappear. When I timed it first in 1960, it took me 55 seconds to go straight up the hill to where the forest road is today and be out of sight. It is only a matter of some 50ft. Here was a bulge in the well-wooded hillside which afforded plenty of cover. At that point, the murderer would have vanished from view, probably turned left and made his way into the large, steep and wooded Gleann a' Chaolais. Once in the shelter of the glen, he could have gone to Ballachulish House or climbed to any vantage point and observed unseen what was happening below. No advantage was to be gained by climbing onto higher ground above the murder spot because this was bare hillside and he would have been seen.

One of the reasons why it has been assumed the shot came from higher on the hillside is simply because in evidence Mungo Campbell said he saw a man wearing a 'short dark-coloured coat with a gun in his hand going away from him ... and he was of so great a distance, that the deponent [Mungo] thinks he could not have known him, tho' he had seen his face'. Such a distance, in fact, that Mungo's first impression was that this figure could not have fired the shot. Later, Mungo changed this opinion, but everything was happening so quickly, and he was in such a fluster, that although he claimed he set off up the hill after the figure, he could not even remember whether it was before or after attending to his dying uncle. The timing here is important.

The figure Mungo saw did not seem in any hurry until Mungo started up the hill after him. It was only then, according to Mungo, that he quickened his pace. The others were on the scene quickly, but as they arrived Mungo had already helped Glenure from his horse, laid him on the ground and was tending to him. If Mungo did run up the very steep hill, then it could have been for only a few strides. The fact that I was out of sight in under a minute tends to suggest the man Mungo saw was much higher. At the point where I disappeared I could easily recognise Inspector Les Liney. Suspicion therefore arises that more than one person was involved.

Les Liney and I discussed matters further. The forensic evidence clearly suggests the shot was fired from low down. From his study of the ground, however, Les also points to the possibility that the man who fired the shot did not run up the hill at all, but merely stepped back into the trees behind him. The contours of the ground, the birches, alders and bushes would swallow him here even quicker. In that case, he could have been out of sight in under ten seconds. It is entirely possible Mungo did not see him. In the time Mungo took to attend to the stricken Glenure the figure would have disappeared.

Ah, but in that case, surely the young servant John Mackenzie would have seen the murderer? Remember, John had fallen behind the others to retrieve the sheriff officer's fallen coat. Young John has been referred to as Glenure's 'loyal servant', but in reality nothing has been known about him. Personally, I have never given him any consideration.

However, information passed to me about young John, during the 250th anniversary events in Appin, forced me to rethink the murder scene entirely. I was the guest of a senior group of Stewarts and their clansmen and had been asked to say a few words of explanation to them about what happened at the murder site. Among the Stewarts present was also a Mackenzie. On hearing of my own passion for the subject, he came over and said that perhaps I would be interested in the fact that he was a descendant of young John. After all these years, I found this astonishing. He then went on to reveal a fascinating tale.

The story of John has also been handed down, generation by generation, in this branch of the Mackenzie family to this day. Apparently, when assassination attempts were planned in Callart, the young Mackenzie remained so close to Glenure that it was impossible to get in a clear shot. This has been recorded in several accounts. Always it has been interpreted as an indication of John's loyalty to Glenure as well as his courage.

It now seems as if sometime before Glenure and his party entered the Wood of Lettermore, John Mackenzie was told to stay well clear of his master. When Kennedy's coat was dropped from his saddle, it could have been inadvertent or by design. Whatever the reason, it had the desired effect of removing Mackenzie. As they passed through the wood, Glenure's assassin was given a clear, uninterrupted and simple shot with Mackenzie, unusually, nowhere to be seen.

If this story is true, and there is no doubting the reliability, conviction or sincerity of the source, then John Mackenzie might very well have seen the assassin but said nothing. Either Mackenzie knew what was going to happen as part of a plot or else the frighteners had been put on him to ensure his silence. The impression I was clearly given was that John Mackenzie's sympathies lay with the Jacobites, and he knew exactly what was going to happen.

All this produces a new picture of what happened. When the terrain, the forensic evidence, the timing, the distances and the Mackenzie factor are all considered together, they tend to indicate the following: the figure seen by Mungo was not the man who fired the shot, which confirms Mungo's original thought. More likely the man Mungo saw was part of the plot, but keeping his head down from higher on the hill, watching what happened. When he heard the shot and saw Glenure crumple, he merely stood up. That was why he did not seem to be in a hurry. The job was done. He could leave the scene at leisure. Whether it was his intention to play a role if the shot had missed or Glenure had been merely winged, we probably will never know.

The real murderer could easily have slipped away in the few seconds Mungo would have been distracted as he attended to his dying uncle. The murderer might even have given the approaching Mackenzie a wave of acknowledgement before making his escape.

The suspicious mind of my detective friend, of course, immediately made a connection with the shooting and the respected figure of Stewart of Ballachulish. It was Stewart of Ballachulish who had met Glenure when he first came off the ferry and they walked chatting together to the entrance of the Wood of Lettermore. Was it by chance or to delay Glenure until the trap was set? It was Stewart of Ballachulish who had called out to John Mackenzie to come back for the dropped coat. It was Stewart of Ballachulish who had a son and nephew, each of whom at various times over the years had been accused of the murder. Coincidences sometimes happen that can be misleading, but had Les Liney been leading the inquiry at the time, he would have wanted to put some hard questions to all of them.

With the help of the youthful Alastair Campbell and his Argylls, and Detective Inspector Les Liney in the present day, I felt we had at least brought greater understanding – if not cast some new light – on what took place in the Wood of Lettermore. But who pulled the trigger?

The name of the man who fired the shot has been a closely-guarded Stewart secret since those two bullets struck home in Glenure's back. Legend says the name of the assassin has been passed down within the clan to this day.

Over the years, around half-a-dozen names have been whispered to me in confidence by people who perhaps could be expected to know something. There have been many others who, with knowing winks and sometimes wise nods, have more or less insinuated: 'I know the name but my lips are sealed'. Most have known nothing. Hearsay, folklore, imagination or even invention have played their parts in naming a name. The Appin Stewarts of 250 years ago, of course, have been scattered to the winds. A whole colony of them found a new home in North Carolina, where they kept the songs, the music, the old traditions of their homeland alive and the tartans flying. Some of it is still reflected in the Grandfather Highland Games there today. I had begun to wonder, however, if anyone was left in Appin who still held the secret.

Then in recent times, I was taking a group of Robert Louis Stevenson Club members around the *Kidnapped* scenes in Appin when we were joined by a senior member of the Stewart clan. Inevitably, I asked this person if they knew the secret name.

'Of course I do, but I'm not going to tell you. It's a Stewart secret.' The reply was matter-of-fact and said with dignity. I tried my list of leading suspects I and others have gathered over the years. There was a firm 'No' to each in turn.

But the statement, coming from this particular Stewart, made me believe it implicitly. Well, well, so more light can still be cast on the mystery, I thought to myself. All it needs is a little more detective work.

9

A Barrowload of Suspects

But when it came to Colin Roy, the black Campbell blood
in him ran wild. He sat gnashing his teeth at the wine table.
What! Should a Stewart get a bite of bread, and him not be
able to prevent it? Ah! Red Fox, if ever I hold you at a
gun's end, the Lord have pity upon ye!

Allan Breck's threat against Colin Campbell in *Kidnapped*

'Okay, so who's on your list of suspects?' asked my detective friend.
'And what exactly happened after Colin Campbell's murder?'

Well, if Appin was tense before the murder, it was worse afterwards,
I explained to former Detective Inspector Les Liney as we examined the case 250 years after the crime. Hate, anger, revenge, fear.
That was what was let loose in Appin. The murder was a terrible
thing – everyone knew and dreaded what the reaction would be
to such an extraordinary act of folly. That is why it is so hard
to believe it was the work of a Stewart to bring such misery to his
own patch.

The Campbells went into top gear within hours. They just took
over as private prosecutors. Resources were flung at the investigation.
Glenure's family were beside themselves with rage. In the higher
echelons of government in London and Edinburgh there was dismay.
But from such a distance, and because uppermost in minds was
concern that this could be the first spark of another Jacobite rebellion,
the situation was misread. King George was informed. Any
possible flame had to be quenched. So Colin Campbell's murder
was presented by the authorities as a major political crime, an insult
to the King, the Hanoverian government, the Campbell clan and
the officers of the law. By the end of the affair, all these factions – one

way or another, some innocently – ganged up to make an example of James Stewart, guilty or innocent.

'Was it really as bad as that? Is that not an exaggerated picture?'

No, I don't think it is. It is difficult to appreciate what a low opinion was held of Highlanders at that time, particularly in the far south. Clansmen were seen as little better than savages. Southerners saw themselves as sophisticated, modernists and reformers. Highlanders, in their view, were an uncouth, retarded breed living in the past and going nowhere.

I waved a favourite quote at Les Liney. Some people in senior circles even saw Glenure's murder as an opportunity to clear up the whole 'nest of vipers' with one swipe. Here is an extract of a letter to General Churchill from Lord Bury at the time: '… it [the murder] is such an Insult upon the government that I hope it will be taken up with a High hand, and not only the murderer brought to Justice but an example made of the whole Clan, Surely the Government can never have a better opportunity of Rooting a Rebellious Clan out of the Country, and peopling it with those whose Loyalty and Zeal for the present Royal Family will be a Terror to their Neighbours … If we are supported in this Affair, it will be the worst shot to the Stewarts they ever made'.

'I hope this isn't an anti-government tirade and a Campbell-bashing session,' said Les Liney. 'Tell me how the murder was viewed among ordinary people.'

Firstly, the powers-that-be in senior government ranks in England also regarded the Campbells with suspicion. They, too, were Highlanders. Even Glenure, their own agent, was suspected of having Jacobite leanings. Campbell-bashing is not the intention here. Had the Stewarts been on the winning side at Culloden, then the Campbells might have received the same treatment. Campbells have had a knack of choosing the right side in history and therefore they are probably Scotland's most successful clan. Sometimes their success has brought jealousy. What I'm telling you is how it was.

Revulsion sums up the reaction of most ordinary people in Appin to the murder. Irrespective of clan loyalties, the cold-blooded killing was seen as a dreadful act. There was much sympathy for Glenure's young wife, Janet, just into her 20s and pregnant, and her two young daughters.

'How quickly did the investigation begin?'

The Campbell prosecutors didn't waste time. The day after the shooting, James Stewart was arrested in the local dram shop at Inshaig, along with his eldest son Allan. James was charged with complicity in the murder, 'art and part' as it was termed. Both were taken to Fort William garrison. Allan was simply held without charge, and his brother Charles joined him shortly afterwards.

Top of the list of suspects was Allan Breck Stewart, James's foster son. He was a well-known Jacobite courier between Scotland and France, French army recruiting officer, close to Ardshiel and a trouble-maker. Allan Breck quickly became Scotland's most wanted man. As the investigation developed, it was soon discovered he was near the murder scene most of the day. He was seen fishing the burn beside

FIGURE 32. Was this the weapon that shot the 'Red Fox'? Former mine host of Edinburgh's Doric Tavern, the late Jimmy McGuffie, believed it to be the 'Black Gun of Misfortune' as it was known in Appin. It was on display in his restaurant for many years, but is now in the safe keeping of the Museum of Scotland. The picture shows the author as a young man discussing the gun's authenticity with Jimmy. However, there are several guns claimed to be the murder weapon.

Ballachulish House, half-a-mile away. At one point he even came down to the ferry to inquire if Glenure had crossed.

'Ah, tell me more about Allan Breck!'

Right, but first let me explain the difference between the real Allan Breck and Robert Louis Stevenson's hero Alan Breck. And Stevenson chose to spell Allan with one 'l', perhaps to draw the distinction. In real life Allan Breck was neither the 'honest Alan ... grim old fire-eater in his day', as referred to in *Catriona*, nor was he the swashbuckling, adventurer swordsman, with the dancing eyes, droll wit and infinite wisdom in *Kidnapped*. There are several other misconceptions to be cleared up between the historical fact and Stevenson's fictional licence. The description of Allan Breck as 'papered' (the issue of a description and reward for his arrest) by James Stewart from his prison cell, was of 'a tall pocked pitted lad with very black hair', about 5ft 10ins and 30 years of age. The *Kidnapped* Alan was short and wiry. A platoon of redcoats accompanied Glenure in *Kidnapped*. In fact, Glenure and his party entered the Wood of Lettermore alone and unarmed. The red-headed Glenure was known as the 'Red Fox' in *Kidnapped*. The term 'Red Fox' was mentioned once in James Stewart's trial by a witness referring to a throwaway remark by Allan Breck after a drinking session. It was by no means certain if the comment even referred to Colin Campbell. The 'Red Fox' was too apt for Stevenson to resist, but it indicates how closely the writer had studied the trial. These small additions to the facts were simply the writer in Stevenson painting in extra colour.

The image of Allan Breck to emerge at the trial was of a lazy, drunken ne'er-do-weel, untrustworthy, a sinister and reckless figure. It was the prosecution's task, of course, to paint as damning a picture as possible, but this image is as likely to have been as exaggerated as Stevenson's.

'Could James have really been involved in the shooting? Was he fairly treated?'

By witnessed location and timing, it was impossible for James Stewart to have played a part at the Wood of Lettermore. Complicity was the only hope the authorities had of sustaining a prosecution. From the moment of his arrest every impediment was put in the way of a fair trial. He was kept in close confinement, which meant no access from the outside. After five weeks, James's wife and daughter were given limited access, but legal representation – or anyone who could have been of help in his plight – was firmly denied. Young John Stewart of Ballachulish made strenuous efforts to rally round James until he was threatened that if he kept meddling he would be arrested.

When a lawyer was eventually found, he proved utterly useless. Charles Stewart was more concerned to remain on good terms with the authorities than look after his client's interests. He was intimidated by both Campbells and the scale of the case. His major concern was that he would be branded one of the 'disaffected' if he did his job too professionally. That meant he would have been viewed as a Jacobite sympathiser. He knew how promising careers could be blighted by that description. Charles Stewart's legal career was therefore far from blighted – and James's legal rights were never pressed.

Stewart of Edinglassie, an able, experienced lawyer, eventually agreed to represent James, but again difficulties were put in his way. By sheer chance, he met James at Tyndrum by the roadside as his client was being taken to Inveraray for trial. But by the time of that brief,

FIGURE 33. The half-submerged rock in the centre of the picture is where Glenure's body was carried after the shooting and taken off by boat. Cloud shadows race over the Ardgour peaks in the background.

accidental encounter, evidence that might have helped James and his lawyer had already been taken. The case of the private prosecutors, the Campbells, was being pursued by a mixture of threats, manipulation, the suppression of both evidence and witnesses. Facts were twisted, witnesses harassed until some altered their original statements.

'Hold it right there! These are serious accusations. Can you really justify them?'

Yes, they certainly are serious. The law was a good deal rougher then than now, of course, and that must be kept in mind, but at the time of the Appin Murder Scotland prided itself on the fairness of its legal system. Even by the standards of 250 years ago, what happened to James Stewart in the run-up to his trial was disgraceful. I don't think there is anyone who would deny it or seek to justify it. It is not too much to say that a substantial part of the evidence presented at James Stewart's trial was achieved by suppression and perjury. It was in this pre-trial period that the seeds of serious miscarriage were sown. The case has been examined by a multitude of legal experts over years. None has argued against this point. One distinguished Scottish High Court judge even called it 'the blackest mark on Scottish legal history'.

'Okay, you've made your point. So tell me what happened to Allan Breck directly after the shooting? On his track record it looks as if the Campbells might have guessed it right.'

Believe me, nothing in this case is certain! Maybe yes, and maybe no. Anyway, after his visit to the ferryman to find out if Glenure had crossed from Callart, Allan Breck was out of sight until he appeared that night (the night of the murder) at the back of Ballachulish House. He asked to speak to Donald Stewart. Yes, the same Donald who was nephew and son-in-law to the Ballachulish laird. Allan Breck swore his innocence to Donald, but asked him to take a message to James Stewart requesting money to get him to France. Appin would now be flooded with soldiers, he said, and as a deserter he dare not show face. He also requested that his good French clothes, which were kept at Acharn, should be brought at the same time. Earlier he had borrowed old clothes from James, and he was wearing these to do work on a neighbour's farm and when he went fishing. These clothes became critical evidence against James.

Allan Breck went on to explain he would make his way to Caolasnacoan, on the south shore of Loch Leven, and hide there until the money arrived. That is exactly what happened. It is known he called in the early hours of the morning at the home of Lady Glencoe to tell her about Glenure's murder. With great difficulty James scraped together five guineas, and had them conveyed to Allan Breck at Caolasnacoan by a local packman called Alexander Stewart.

'Right, now what about the trial? How did they find an unbiased jury in Campbell country? Given the political dimensions, were the judges fair?'

The conduct of the trial was generally handled in a proper manner. Of course, it was held at Inveraray, the seat of the Clan Campbell, which gave it home advantage. It also has to be said that if the unfortunate James Stewart had been afforded better legal advice in the first instance, he might have had his case heard in Edinburgh. Would it have made a difference? Possibly. A short time before James was tried, Edinburgh juries acquitted two Jacobites in separate trials. In the case of James Stewart, however, the prosecution decided to eliminate any chance of an acquittal by ensuring the trial was heard in Argyll. In that heavily-biased setting anything other than a hanging would have been a surprise.

Few chances were taken with the jury either. In mitigation, it has to be said that in Argyll it was never going to be easy to find any suitable juror who was not a Campbell or associated with the clan. As it turned out, of the 15 jurors sitting in judgement on James, 11 of them were Campbells. The presiding judge was the Duke of Argyll himself, the head of the Clan Campbell. Unusually, especially in a case against a Stewart, the senior judge carried not only the clout of the court, but also the power of the Clan Chief. On pain of punishment, clan tradition was to follow the wishes of the chief. Argyll's hatred of Jacobites was well known.

'So James wasn't given much of a chance really, was he?'

James felt the rope round his neck from the moment he heard of Glenure's death. But in their rush to hang James Stewart and catch Allan Breck, the authorities, in my view, did a further disservice to justice. They looked no further. There were several other lines of inquiry screaming to be investigated. They were not pursued.

The trial was set for Thursday, September 21, four months after the murder. It was designed to display the full might and majesty of the law. Redcoat soldiers paraded, the drums were beating, Inveraray

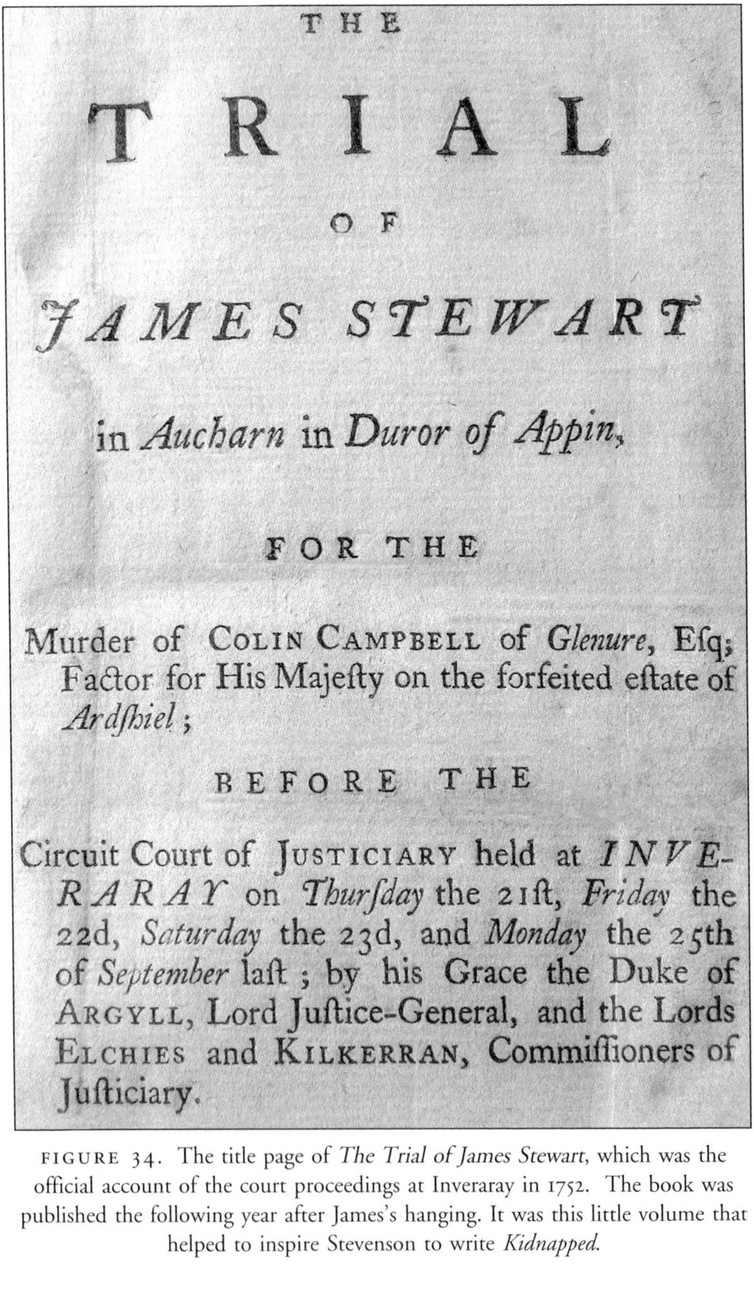

THE

TRIAL

OF

JAMES STEWART

in *Aucharn* in *Duror* of *Appin*,

FOR THE

Murder of COLIN CAMPBELL of *Glenure*, Efq;
Factor for His Majefty on the forfeited eftate of
Ardfhiel;

BEFORE THE

Circuit Court of JUSTICIARY held at *INVE-
RARAY* on *Thurfday* the 21ft, *Friday* the
22d, *Saturday* the 23d, and *Monday* the 25th
of *September* laft ; by his Grace the Duke of
ARGYLL, Lord Juftice-General, and the Lords
ELCHIES and KILKERRAN, Commiffioners of
Jufticiary.

FIGURE 34. The title page of *The Trial of James Stewart*, which was the
official account of the court proceedings at Inveraray in 1752. The book was
published the following year after James's hanging. It was this little volume that
helped to inspire Stevenson to write *Kidnapped*.

was packed. It was before the present attractive new town of Inveraray was built, but the crumbling old town boasted both a church and jail. James was accommodated in the jail and his trial was held in the church. Sitting with the Duke were the two respected and experienced judges, Patrick Grant of Elchies and Sir James Fergusson of Kilkerran.

The first opportunity James's lawyer was given to sit down with his client and full defence team was September 19. James's lawyer asked for character witnesses to be admitted, including James's good friend, the respected Donald Campbell of Airds. The Duke's response set the political agenda from the outset. 'Would you pretend, sir, to prove the moral character of the accused after his being guilty of rebellion, a crime that comprehends all other crimes. Here you will find treason, murders, rapines, oppressions, perjuries, etc', declared the Duke. Character witnesses for James were therefore refused and it was as good as a nod to the Campbell jurors.

'With everything set against him, what kind of defence was James Stewart able to present?'

Quite strong, I would say, at least in a normal situation. In spite of James's inadequate legal preparations, his preliminary defence seemed sound. Basically, it claimed James could not be convicted as an accessory to a murder committed by someone else until the murderer himself had been caught and convicted. For example, if Allan Breck had later been caught, tried and found not guilty, James would already have been executed. If Allan Breck was not guilty, there was no case against James. This argument was also disallowed. At that point, the prosecutors were more interested in hanging James than catching Allan Breck. Had Allan Breck been captured, it might have been embarrassing.

The trial itself, however, was not unfairly conducted. Apart from the Duke of Argyll's prejudice against Stewarts and Jacobites, and a disgraceful speech for the crown by Simon Fraser, Lord Advocate William Grant of Prestongrange and the judges involved dealt properly with the facts that were put before them. It was what had gone on in advance of the trial that disfigured the whole case. The 'short dark coat' worn by the man on the hillside, as described by Mungo Campbell, Glenure's nephew, is worth mentioning. Allan Breck was wearing clothes of an entirely different description when fishing on the same day. Mungo was not even asked for his description in court. Any evidence that might point the finger away from Allan Breck could weaken or collapse the case against James.

It is interesting, too, that the significant evidence given by the witness John Breck Maccoll, the 'bouman' at Caolasnacoan, about the threats made by Allan Breck on Glenure's life, were not provided until around seven weeks and several interviews later. Maccoll had been arrested for his part in assisting in Allan Breck's escape and therefore was in serious trouble. After his revealing evidence no further action was taken against him.

'Did James ever waver about his innocence? Was there no confession or a pointing finger at the time of his execution?'

No, he met his fate with enormous dignity. James's bad luck continued to the end so that even the weather for his hanging was against him. It was a filthy day of wind and rain. A large guard of redcoat soldiers provided an intimidating show of force, a crowd of local people gathered and a tent had been erected for last prayers.

The Dying Speech was the fashion of the day then, and some Jacobites used it to score political points. In James's case, his Dying Speech was restrained, dignified and solemn. James denied he had been involved in Colin Campbell's murder, directly or indirectly, or that he knew whose hand had fired the shot. He prayed that God would pardon the jury and the false witnesses so that they would not be charged with his innocent blood.

For a man of James Stewart's religious principles, had such a statement at such a time been false, his soul would have been consigned to purgatory. He knew this very well and therefore his words carry the ring of truth. It is entirely conceivable that James would have been the last person to know if there was a plot. Every action James took to save the Appin tenants from eviction was by working inside and with the law. Those involved in a plot, if there was one, would have known he would try to talk them out of it. It was better that James, of all people, knew nothing.

Before mounting the steps to the gallows, James knelt and read a prayer. It was said to be Psalm 35. It has been known in Appin ever since as Salm Seumas a' Ghlinne: 'False witnesses did rise up: they laid to my charge things that I knew not ...'

'That's a very sad end to the matter. But now tell me more about Allan Breck.'

Yes, Allan Breck clearly deserves closer examination. He was the son of Donald Stewart, of Inverchromie in Rannoch, who had his own problems with the law. He handed Allan over to James Stewart as a foster son. In reality, in spite of the reprehensible figure depicted at the trial, Allan Breck must have been a man of some capability. After all, he was Ardshiel's courier between France and Appin, and to carry out such a task called for trust and guile. During his army service for France, Allan Breck received the Cross of Military Merit, which rewarded non-Catholic foreigners with an honour equal to the Order of St Louis. It seems Allan Breck was not lacking in courage. He was also decorated as a Chevalier of Military Merit, which provided him with a pension, and he had a further pension from Bouillon's Regiment. We know he vanished into the heather three days after the Glenure killing, but didn't arrive in France until some 10 months later. Where was he? We don't know for sure.

'What happened to him in later life? Did he ever return to Scotland?'

At the age of 68, in 1790, it is understood he had accommodation in the Rue de la Harpe, in Paris.

There were other sightings and opportunities for the truth to come out. Alexander Campbell of Ardchattan, an ancestor of Alastair Campbell of Airds' wife, recounted in a letter how on a visit to Paris in 1787, he met a tall, thin, ugly man who said he came from Appin. He said his name was Allan Breck and was suspected of murdering Ardchattan's uncle, Colin Campbell. He swore by all that was sacred to him that he played no part. However, he knew who did it, he said, but was bound by oath to keep the secret. The truth was in his papers, he said, to be revealed when he died. Someone must have got there first because apparently nothing was found.

It is possible Sir Walter Scott knew the secret. In the introduction to *Rob Roy*, the shooting of Glenure and its aftermath are outlined by Scott, who then speculated about the attempted abduction of Allan Breck by James More Drummond or MacGregor, the rogue son of Rob Roy. Scott gives an account similar to Ardchattan's. An unidentified friend of Scott's had been in Paris and discovered a 'tall, thin, raw-boned, grim-looking old man' with a sunburned and

FIGURE 35. Caught unawares ... it is dramach and cheese time which demands full concentration from the author. He spent a few days in 1960 in the Wood of Lettermore to allow his blisters to recover.

heavily-freckled face. He, too, claimed to be Allan Breck. Scott's father, as a Writer to the Signet, had access to the estate of Dougal Stewart, one of the Appin Stewart chiefs, who in turn had a strong friendship with Alexander Stewart of Invernahyle, the factor of Appin at the time of the murder. Invernahyle was a visitor to the Scott household and the young Walter spent a holiday in Appin with Invernahyle in 1786. Surely he could not have failed to discuss the murder. Confidentiality was more respected then than now, which could account for Scott avoiding the subject in his writing. Robert Louis Stevenson, of course, was the beneficiary.

'Allan Breck troubles me. Where was he from the time he visited the ferryman until his appearance at Ballachulish House? There's no satisfactory answer. Allan Breck had the motive, he had access to firearms, he had knowledge of the country and the movements of the victim, he had the guts to do it and he had the skill of the soldier. But there are some things here that just don't add up.'

Now it was my turn to put a question. Come on then, Les, said I. What's not making sense?

'I don't think it would be his style. If Allan Breck contemplated an assassination, he would have had his escape meticulously planned. Money, food, clothes and a route would have been ready. He would have pulled the trigger, stood up, lifted his well-organised getaway gear – and simply vanished. As it was, after the shot, Allan Breck had no money, no provisions, he didn't dare visit James and he was forced to skulk for three days waiting for the means of his escape to be delivered. To draw attention to himself at the ferry hours before the murder was hardly the action of a professional. Allan Breck's continuous assertion of innocence, even to close friends, is difficult to understand if it isn't true. He was a bit of a braggart, it seems, yet in France where he could have boasted about his fine shot, he consistently repeated his innocence. Of course, without firm evidence, who can tell now? He could well be guilty.'

Agreed, said I, so let me try another scenario. Let me tell you about the plot theory. Here is a story that first came to light in the Dewar Manuscripts, which is a collection of tales collected by John Dewar, a woodman employed by the 8th Duke of Argyll. Dewar sought out these traditional stories of the Highlands and folklore about a century after the murder. His story tells of a shooting match held by a group of Appin conspirators at a lonely spot called Lochan Blar nan Lochan, up above Bealach, between Salachan Glen and Loch Creran. It was agreed, says the story, that the best marksman would shoot Glenure and the best gun would be the weapon. The named assassin in this story is Donald Stewart, nephew and son-in-law of Alexander Stewart of Ballachulish, the same Alexander Stewart who spoke with Glenure before he entered the Wood of Lettermore. Donald lived with his uncle and cousin John in Ballachulish House. The gun belonged to Dugald MacColl, one of James Stewart's servants, who made an exceedingly nervous witness at the trial. Of course, the problem again is lack of evidence. It could be true, but it could be no more than folk-tale.

'It's feasible.'

Ah, but it gets more complicated! Donald Stewart's cousin John was also the name that was once whispered to me as the man who fired the shot and killed Colin Campbell. I was told by the Reverend Somerled Macmillan, the former Free Church minister in Ballachulish, around 1945. I wrote about it and the account was published in the old *Weekly Scotsman* in the 1960s. I can tell you, Mr Macmillan firmly and sincerely believed John Stewart was the secret name of the murderer, just as he believed the name of the murderer was being passed down through generations of a small group of Stewarts in the area.

'If there was a conspiracy, with Allan Breck's background you could almost bet he would be in on it or know about it. Maybe that's why in France he said he was innocent but knew who did it. If Donald Stewart was the assassin, or another senior Stewart, I suppose it could have been agreed that Allan Breck took the blame. He was a bird of passage, he would be an immediate suspect and he was leaving the country anyway.'

Exactly, but that would turn Allan Breck into a kind of hero. If it's true, it was an unselfish act because it meant he could never return to Appin. It might have been hoped his disappearance would take the heat off the others, and that's what happened. The prosecutors didn't look for anyone else.

'It would also account for showing himself at the ferry. He would be trying to draw attention to himself. But again, why would he have been so disorganised?' commented Les Liney.

Okay, but what if while he was out fishing he saw something suspicious and stumbled on to the assassination by others, known or unknown? As soon as the bullets struck Glenure, Allan Breck knew he would have to quit Appin fast. And that is the story he gave to Donald Stewart on the evening of the murder.

'That makes sense, too. It would explain his total unpreparedness for escape,' said Les.

Let me try you with yet another scenario. On the night of May 13, that's the day before the murder, four Camerons were known to have slipped across the ferry into Appin. Nothing more was heard of them. That in itself was suspicious at the time because Appin was well populated then. Remember, too, the Cameron grudge against Glenure was just as intense as the Stewarts'. For Camerons it would make sense to shoot Glenure outside Cameron country. Let others take the blame. And after the trial, it is claimed, a Cameron snatch team offered to ambush the military escort taking James Stewart from Inveraray to Fort William to spring him. James himself declined this handsome gesture from the Camerons, it is said. It would bring more grief to his clan than his life was worth. James had originally set the hares running by suggesting the murder could have been the work of the formidable Sergeant More Cameron, well-known Campbell hater, but he had not been seen for about a year. At the time, in Cameron country, there was a general belief that this desperate character had a hand in it. Cameron plots against Glenure were common talk, and the suspicion against them is not to be dismissed lightly.

'Well, that, too, has the ring of possibility. But is it true? Like the others, is there evidence? The Cameron theory would certainly have needed thorough investigation to eliminate them from enquiries.'

I'm coming to the end of my list of possible suspects and explanations, you'll be glad to hear. But I must mention Red Ewan MacColl, who was an early suspect, mostly because he fitted the description, given by Mungo Campbell, of the man on the hillside at Lettermore. Red Ewan's dress was a near-perfect match. He was given a cast-iron alibi by being at a meeting four miles away in Glencoe at the time, but were his friends telling the truth?

There has also been linkage to the unsavoury Robin Oig, murderer, abductor and son of the famous Rob Roy and brother of the scheming James More. Robin Oig has been named in some quarters as the hitman. The theory seems to stem from a letter from Campbell of Barcaldine to the Barons Exchequer in Edinburgh, suggesting James Stewart had tried to bribe Robin Oig by offering him passage to France, where he would be looked after by Ardshiel, the Appin Stewart captain. All Robin Oig had to do in exchange was remove Glenure at the end of a gun. Barcaldine, Glenure's half-brother, was tending to ride roughshod over truth and law at the time in his rush to get a conviction. It's like so many of these stories: how much faith do you put in it?

Now, to my knowledge, you know just about everything! A pretty parcel of murderers, rogues and ruffians. So whodunnit, Mr Detective? I could see Les Liney take a long swallow.

'I haven't the slightest idea! I don't think I've ever encountered a case with so many twists and turns. I hesitate even to speculate. In any event, the trail is cold. If I had to put money on any one of the suspects, I would have to say Allan Breck. One way or another, he was involved or was in the know. And the Camerons! If only we knew more about the Camerons. Frankly, in my view, the only way it's possible now to find out who shot Colin Campbell is to get one of these Stewarts you mention, the ones who've had the secret name passed down to them for the last 250 years, to spill the beans. Frankly, that sounds a bit of a tall story, too. They may not be so easy to find.'

I was thinking so myself, said I. And Les wished me well for the next stage of my inquiries.

10

The Flight in the Heather

How Allan Breck and David Balfour visited the House of Fear, took the high road into the mountains, jumped for their lives across a foaming river, 'birstled' on a rock like scones on a girdle, and I make my home in Murder Wood, meet a world champion piper, and find myself 'blind' in the mist.

Sleeping in the open at a murder site may not be to everyone's taste, but when I first tramped the *Kidnapped* Way in 1960, I didn't give it a thought. In any event, when I arrived in the Wood of Lettermore, I was too tired after my exertions from Kingairloch, and all my concentration was focused on my feet. During the night I was conscious at various intervals of serenading owls, and when I woke I startled a pair of roe deer, which charged up that very hillside where Glenure's assassin lay in wait.

Feet were my first priority and the blisters forced me to alter my plans. It was another splendid, warm day, blue sky, light breeze, and with it the midges vanished like magic. Billions were lurking in the wood waiting for their next victim, but at that moment they had disappeared as completely as Allan Breck after the murder. I dressed my feet, pulled on socks and boots. Aah! The blisters complained, but not as loudly as I expected.

I took stock. Here I was where I longed to be, as Stevenson might have said, in Appin Murder country with all those well-known sites recorded in *Kidnapped* waiting to be examined. The Wood of Lettermore is about halfway between Cnap a' Chaolais, where James Stewart was hanged, and Glen Duror, where he lived. The weather was settled, time was mine, and from experience I knew I had to give the blisters a chance to heal before the next part of my journey, which was going to be high, lonely and rough. I therefore decided the Wood of Lettermore would be my home for a few days and, to make it easy on my feet, I planked my rucksack and caught the bus for the few minutes' journey into Ballachulish and then to Duror in the opposite direction.

The 'House of Fear', James Stewart's old home of Acharn in Glen Duror, was my first call, although it gave me more walking than intended. Remember how David and Allan came off the hillside at nightfall after the murder? Below them they saw lighted brands, grasped by shadowy, scurrying figures, as James Stewart's people frantically tried to conceal weapons from the search they knew would be coming. Allan whistled three times, in a special way, and the lights halted immediately, then moved on again as the signal was recognised. James was in a panic, burning papers, wringing his hands, biting his fingers. His wife sat by the fire and wept. One of his sons burned a paper that James felt should have been kept, and James cried out: 'Are ye gone gyt [mad]? Do you wish to hang your father?' With that his wife threw her apron over her head and sobbed even louder.

Acharn was a ruin when I first called and nowadays it has collapsed entirely. James Stewart's old home, once a series of farm buildings, is now little more than a pile of stones. It was interesting to see here, however, how Stevenson muddied historical accuracy by slipping in some of his writer's licence. Firstly, in real life, Allan Breck did not return to Acharn after the murder. Secondly, it would have taken the whistle of a steam train to be heard at Acharn from the hillside described by Stevenson. Unless Allan and David made a long and pointless detour, the landscape doesn't match the *Kidnapped* description without a pole vault of imagination. In *Kidnapped* Allan Breck also collected his 'good' French clothes at Acharn, whereas in fact they were sent to him at Caolasnacoan and were referred to in evidence. These are perhaps trivial matters and Appin was not particularly well known to Stevenson. For the sake of the story, however, it was important that David Balfour – and the reader – met James Stewart face to face, the hub figure in both *Kidnapped* and *Catriona*, and was offered a revealing glimpse inside that tragic household before his arrest.

Stevenson came to Appin to research *Kidnapped* in 1882. Tantalisingly, only one page of a note on *Kidnapped* exists, which was misdated by Stevenson as 1880. 'It was the last of many journeys with my father,' he wrote in the note. 'It was the first time I had travelled with him since we were at all on a footing of equality. The weather was very wild; we were confined whole days to the inn parlour, at Glenorchy, at Oban and elsewhere, but the time sped with that delightful comrade. I have rarely been well received among strangers, never if they were womenfolk; and I recall how it pleased and amused me to be a sharer in my father's popularity, and in the public sitting rooms to be the centre of delightful groups of girls: the stormy and tender old man with the noble mouth and great luminous eyes, had, almost to the end, so great a gift of pleasing. At Ballachulish we had no difficulty in finding the cairn that still marks the place of death; and when we inquired after ...'

Here the note ends abruptly. It isn't even clear how the Stevensons travelled to Appin, if or how long they stayed or where. It was the original idea to make a base at Lochearnhead and push out from there, but they probably changed their plans as they travelled. It is known they found accommodation in Glenorchy for a day or two, as the note confirms, and if they ventured across Rannoch Moor from this point it would have been a rough and difficult trip to Glencoe by stage. Stevenson would have been anxious to check the Moor's landscape, and therefore perhaps they did take the stage, which would explain those atmospheric descriptions. Of course, from Glenorchy they could have reached Appin through Oban by either stage or boat. It was Stevenson's way, of course, to write from memory, and *Kidnapped* was scratched out around four years later in Bournemouth. Sometimes Stevenson's memory let him down, but sometimes he altered things as if to say 'I am not going to let my story be inhibited by minor detail', and sometimes he changed things just to remind readers that *Kidnapped* was fiction and not fact. Sometimes it is difficult to distinguish one reason from another.

Off the main road, Appin looks rather as it was when that assassin's shot echoed around the hills. On the main road it's all change. There is the same people movement, the same mixtures, the same innovations and the same casualties among ancient traditions as in other parts of the Highlands. But the tourist stakes are high in Appin, and because the area is rich in history and visitors like history, serious attempts have been taken to reflect Appin's past. The thriving Appin

Historical Society has played a role here and nowadays there is a properly signposted 'Kidnapped' Trail, which is well tramped.

Ardshiel House, home of Charles Stewart, the chief who led the Appin Stewarts at Culloden, was rebuilt after the ravages of the hated Captain Caroline Scott. Since then it has been both a private house and, latterly, a fine country house hotel of the old, gracious Scottish style, furnishings and comfort, with splendid grounds looking over Loch Linnhe. In recent times, until his tragic death in a helicopter accident in Appin, the owner was Neil Sutherland, formerly a Queen's Own Cameron Highlanders officer, later secretary of the Royal Hong Kong Jockey Club. Ardshiel was his boyhood retreat and he fell in love with its setting and history. Ardshiel is that kind of house. Unfortunately, it passed out of his family, but such was the sense of loss that Neil vowed some day to win it back. That is how it worked out and he returned to where he felt he belonged. Presumably he owned a pair of trousers, but I never saw them. He was a kilt-wearer since childhood, which fitted very well into the home of a Stewart chief. At one time there was an Ardshiel House in Hong Kong, the residence of Colonial Secretary James Stewart Lockhart, who once lived in the original Ardshiel. The name continues as an upmarket Hong Kong estate.

Ballachulish House, where Allan Breck appeared on the evening of the murder, is also a high-quality private hotel. The yew tree, where the 'black gun of misfortune' was found, still stands a few yards away. One glance up Gleann a' Chaolais behind, leading up to the rocks and escarpments of the Beinn a' Bheithir ridge, explains why it would have been so difficult to locate Allan Breck. Trout still rise in the burn beside the hotel where Allan went fishing on the day of the murder, but the only fishing done these days is for errant golf balls from the surrounding golf course.

James Stewart's bones, peaceful at last, lie in the quiet of Keil Church, beside Loch Linnhe. The former Stewart stronghold of Castle Stalker in Loch Laich remains an eye-stopper, and the last time I visited the nearby Culloden Memorial, where the terrible toll of Stewarts is recorded, there was a woman weeping.

I returned to Appin for the 250th commemorative service marking the anniversary of 'Crochadh Seumas a' Ghlinne', the hanging of James of the Glen. It had been organised by the Stewart Society at Cnap a' Chaolais, beside the monument erected by the Stewarts in 1911, where

FIGURE 36. Let us remember ... the scene at the service in November, 2002, to mark the 250th anniversary of James Stewart of the Glen's execution. The monument behind marks the place where the 30ft-high gallows stood. Part of the inscription reads, 'hanged for a crime of which he was not guilty'. The service was conducted by the Rev. Kenneth Wigston, the former Glencoe and Ballachulish Episcopal minister, and part of it was in Gaelic. The piper in the background is Angus MacColl, one of the top ten pipers in the world.

the gibbet stood and James Stewart bravely met his end. The big stone on top of the monument came from James's old home at Acharn. David Stewart of Achara led the modern-day service, conducted partly in Gaelic by the Rev. Kenneth Wigston, the former Glencoe and Ballachulish Episcopal minister, and a piper played Stewart laments in the background, including the White Banner. It was a small gathering, not more than 25, and some of those were media people, recording the event but hoping, on such a special anniversary, that the name of Glenure's murderer would at last be revealed.

It was not revealed – and I was glad. Three times during that service James Stewart's innocence was declared, not as a hero or with bitterness, but merely as a statement of fact. It was not a particularly moving service, nothing sentimental, thank goodness, past clan enmity went unremarked and there was passing reference only to Colin Campbell of Glenure. Nor was there regret about the death of Colin, and that may have been a tiny, defiant warpipe skirl from the past. The silent mountains were eloquent enough for most of us there. It struck me Colin Campbell's assassination had taken place when Appin was dressed in its spring green, but six months later Seumas a' Ghlinne's last sight was of the gold and tawny Appin of late autumn.

I shut my eyes and listened to the piper. It is the tragedy of good performers that they go half-heard when their art is performed at public gatherings. But when I concentrated on his playing, I suddenly thought – hey, this is some piper! I hadn't heard the pipes played like that for many a year. Later, I asked his name and he said it was Angus MacColl. Then I understood!

Angus MacColl is one of the top ten pipers in the world, and the latest of a long and distinguished line of piping MacColls spanning 200 years and more. His family are among the last of the original Appin folk still living in the area. The wee village store at Duror, which bears the MacColl name, has been in the family for at least 80 years – and I had bought my cheese, raisins and chocolate there 40 years ago. The famous John MacColl, piping legend from the nineteenth century, was Angus's great grand-uncle. John won the piper's coveted gold medal at Inverness in 1900 and Angus won gold in 2000, and indeed is a three-times winner, with maybe more to come.

It is interesting how many people who achieve a touch of greatness in their lives are so unassuming and easy. Angus is one of the few in

Appin whose family can bridge the centuries between the days of James Stewart and modern times. His ancestors swung their claymores with the Appin Regiment. Piping of his quality has taken him around the world, and he is recognised as one of the great piping teachers, but he still works the family croft. It is a life not far removed from those who went before him. I asked if he knew the name of the Appin assassin. 'No I don't,' he said. 'The MacColls and Stewarts are close, and there were MacColls cited as witnesses at James Stewart's trial, but even then few people knew the name. It certainly hasn't been handed down in my family.'

On that first trek in David Balfour's footsteps, I returned to the Wood of Lettermore each evening to sleep. At daybreak I would take my ablutions at Loch Linnhe side. Wash, shave, steel myself and plunge in. I even did a washing during those few days of rest and hung it out to dry, out of sight, and no one was the wiser. I ate well, too. In a grocer's shop in Ballachulish village I bought bread, bacon, half-a-dozen eggs to fry and hard-boil on my primus. I lived like a laird. And my feet were improving. My washing and cooking area was behind the big rock where I had been attacked by that cloud of midges. I learned later it was the rock where Colin Campbell's body had been brought to be taken off by boat. Such is the link between past and present!

With my blisters uncomplaining, my next overnight stop on the *Kidnapped* Trail was to be the farm of Caolasnacoan, about eight miles away, beside Loch Leven, and behind the Pap of Glencoe. That was where Allan Breck hid while he waited for James Stewart to send his escape money. There is no mystery about this or how Allan made his way there. He had to get out of sight fast and therefore he took the shortest route. For Allan Breck to move unseen at night in his own country was child's play. He could have clung more or less to the lochside or just above it and made reason-able speed. Robert Louis Stevenson, however, decided that was too simple for David Balfour and his Allan Breck. To add excitement to his story, Stevenson decided to route his heroes up mountains, down passes, have them leap foaming rivers, and encounter redcoats in the middle of Glencoe.

In his letter of instruction for the *Kidnapped* map, Stevenson is clear-cut about the route: 'Thence along the hilltops to Duror: full.

Thence up S side of the River Duror, and the N side of the river Creran, and over Beinn Maol Chaluim and across the Coe below Meannarclach: dotted. Then round the outside of the hilltops above the Coe and then above Loch Leven to a place above Caolasnacoan: full'.

He was still sticking to his dotted and full line to indicate the wandering, fictional trek. To say this route is challenging is an understatement. And it was done at night. A bristling mass of mountains, deep, rock-strewn valleys, grim gullies, foaming chasms, rearing rock towers, canyons and dramatic mountain shapes await all who enter this heaving wilderness. Some of the cliffs have overhangs, some of the hillsides are stoneshoots, some of the classic rock climbs in Scotland beckon. This is almost SAS stuff. Every year bodies are taken off these hills.

FIGURE 37. It was through these unforgiving Glencoe mountains that David and Allan made their desperate bid to evade the Appin Murder manhunt. Allan took a wrong turning in the night-time flight, which could have brought them out around this point in the glen. The picture shows Gearr Aonach and Aonach Dubh with the nose of Bidian nam Bian in the background. Stevenson does not make it clear where the fugitives emerged and adopts writer's licence to muddy the location.

The historical fact is that Allan Breck took the opposite direction, low along the loch rather than high into the mountains. Stevenson was well aware of Allan Breck's route but chose to ignore it. Presumably the lure of the hills was too powerful, and the mountains also provided a further fertile adventure ground for his imagination. It is easy to understand Stevenson's logic. His route from Lettermore to Acharn makes sense in keeping his heroes out of sight. It is rough, bare, wet and exposed terrain up there, but David and Allan could move unseen in the 'dead' ground. Reaching Beinn Maol Chaluim was also a reasonable objective, I thought, as a useful signpost for the reader. After that Stevenson's route is baffling. In the exposed middle of Glencoe, with the redcoats closing in, Allan Breck provides a simple explanation. 'I have proved myself a gommeral this night,' said Allan. 'First of all I take a wrong road, and that in my own country in Appin; so that the day has caught us where we should never have been; and thanks to that we lie here in some danger and mair discomfort.'

But what wrong road, and what was the right one? Stevenson has us guessing. His 'dotted line' on the map neatly disguises the exact spot. Maybe in Bournemouth he was still working on his small-scale map. The one-time shieling of Meannarclach is mentioned halfway down Glencoe, which was full of redcoats (as in fact it soon was after the murder). David and Allan could not risk discovery by moving through the glen to Caolasnacoan, so this chancy location forced them upwards, a dizzy climb on to the jagged ridge of the Aonach Eagach, where the map line is shown straight and full along its top.

Even the SAS might jib at climbing up there at night without good cause. The Aonach is one of the great ridge walks in Scotland. A long, arduous and exposed scramble in good weather, with some excitement clambering over its pinnacles, but at night it is for the experienced only. All the toe and handholds are in place, but the floor of the glen is 2,000 feet below, and at several places the track is no more than a foot or two wide. If Allan and David had travelled on the 'outside' of the ridge, as Stevenson's map suggested, in parts they would have walked on air.

I decided to head out on the Stevenson route and play it safe. The weather was changing again, I was on my own and these big mountains are not to be toyed with. I packed my gear in the Wood of Lettermore, left never a trace of my presence, patted the murder cairn as I passed, and headed up the hill. It is interesting to know that the small, vicious rock face just above and to the right of the cairn is now a testing ground for mountaineering hard men. In recent times I met up with former Glencoe Mountain Rescue Team leader Davie Gunn, who told me some of the pitches on that fierce face have been named from *Kidnapped*: the Red Fox, graded extreme, and the Covenant, after Captain Hoseason's brig Covenant, will test the best.

My plan was to follow Stevenson's instructions to the point where I would have to descend into Glen Duror to reach Acharn. Usually I climbed light, carrying only a spare jumper and rations, so I found my 40lb rucksack a real sweat, and having gained height I was reluctant to lose it again. I could traverse the flanks of Beinn a' Bheithir and make my way round to the ridge above Glen Duror until I was overlooking Glen Creran. Below me was the cave where Charles Stewart, the Appin chief, hid before his escape to France, although he also had several other hidey-holes in the area. I had an eagle's-eye view of those farms whose names were recorded in the Appin tragedy – Lagnaha, Achindarroch and the rubble of James Stewart's old home of Acharn.

By the time I reached the ridge and looked down into Glen Creran, the view was clear but I could see the crests of the big tops misting over. My easiest route was to drop down to the River Creran and follow it upstream, dodging high ground because my pack seemed to be getting heavier the longer I carried it, and heading up Bealach Caol Creran, past the three waterfalls, then slogging upwards again through Bealach Clach nam Meirleach to Coire Cearcaill. When I stood on the coire my face was like an over-ripe tomato, the back of my shirt soaked in sweat and the mist was settling in thick on the tops.

I followed the infant Allt Charnan burn until I was immediately below Beinn Maol Chaluim where I made a decision. Beinn Maol Chaluim is not a Munro because it falls around 300 feet short of the 3,000-ft requirement, but I was dismayed at how big and steep it looked. There was no way I was going to lug my big pack up there! I was losing speed, and if I were not careful I could become exhausted up there in the back of beyond; fingers of mist were trailing across the hillside in front of my nose. Allan Breck and David Balfour travelled light, and so would I. The answer was simple – plank my pack and return for it. It is a perfectly sound tactic so long as it can be found again. I stuck some chocolate in my anorak and climbed upwards.

Halfway up I wondered why on earth Allan and David had come this way. It was a fair pech and I was climbing blind. When at last I stood on the top of Beinn Maol Chaluim I saw – nothing! I knew there was an array of mountains all around. I was looking on to the southern face of Bidean nam Bian, Sgor na h-Ulaidh was behind me, a mass of rocks and gullies before me led on to the three grim sisters above the Glencoe road, the long ridge of the Buachaille Etive Beag and the massive rock walls of the Buachaille Etive Mor were somewhere to my right – but I could see not a thing. Mist distorts shapes, and as it thickens and swirls it seems to create its own eerie shapes. It is a time to be wary. It was a major disappointment because from the summit I hoped to work out the route Stevenson had in mind for his intrepid travellers. It was not to be. The mist was not going to lift. It was time to get off the top. And I have never been back.

I found my rucksack without difficulty. The wet mist was lowering and chilling, there was no shelter, Coire Cearcail looked uninviting and I decided to seek an escape route out of the mountains. Playing it safe remains one of the key rules on Scottish mountains, and although I was in absolutely no danger on that walk, it was nonetheless time to go. The easy answer would have been to drop down into Glen Etive, but that was taking me in the wrong direction. Caolasnacoan, on the far end of the Aonach Eagach, remained my target.

After a careful study of the map – and a groan at the prospect of more climbing – I decided to heave my rucksack up Bealach Fhionnghaill, below the rocks of Craig Dubh, an outrider of Beinn Maol Chaluim, and head for the Fionn Ghleann. I knew it would bring me out into the long Gleann Leac na Muidhe, where some of the Glencoe MacDonalds made their escape in the snow after the massacre. Across the River Coe at the mouth of the glen there were sheltering woods, which I knew well, and I now had these in mind as a place to spend the night.

But where in Glencoe did Allan and David leap for their lives across the thundering river? Where did they climb to safety on top of those 20ft-high rocks that leaned together, while the redcoats bayoneted the heather around them? Where were their locations?

FIGURE 38. Hang or drown! A dramatic moment in Glencoe caught by the artist W. Boucher as Allan and David flee for their lives. The waterfall places the incident at what is known as the Study in the middle of the glen, but Stevenson is vague about the exact spot. On this section of the march Stevenson alters locations for the sake of his story and this leap for life could have been much lower in the valley. *The Writers' Museum, Edinburgh*

The scene as David and Allan jumped the River Coe was nerve-wracking, the white water roaring and swirling around them, with a sense of water kelpies waiting for a slip:

> So there we stood, side by side upon a small rock slippery with spray, a far broader leap in front of us, and the river dinning on all sides," said David. "When I saw where I was, there came on me a deadly sickness of fear, and I put my hand over my eyes. Alan took me and shook me; I saw he was speaking, but the roaring of the falls and the trouble of my mind prevented me from hearing; only I saw his face was red with anger, and that he stamped upon the rock ... Then, putting his hands to his mouth and his mouth to my ear, he shouted, 'Hang or drown!' and turning his back upon me, leaped over the further branch of the stream, and landed safely.

I have walked both banks of this short river several times and never found a satisfactory spot. It has been suggested Stevenson had in mind the Glencoe upstream waterfall at the place known as The Study as the site of this adventure. If this were the case, it would have meant David and Allan had exited from that jungle of mountains by the Lairig Eilde or Coirre Gabhail, the Lost Valley, as it is known to generations of climbers. Stevenson does not mention or describe a waterfall in the text and I always took 'the roaring of the falls' to mean the river in spate, as the snow on the hills melts, when there are countless little falls and some of them certainly roar when the Coe is high.

Those fine artists J. B. Hole, N. C. Wyeth and Dudley Watkins, whose illustrations have graced various editions of *Kidnapped*, also fail to define the location. Hole's drawing of the tiny figure about to make his leap across the raging torrent is perhaps most like the Glencoe falls, but really it could be anywhere. They, too, have sensibly used their own artistic licence to dodge the exact location, and quite right.

As it happens, the River Coe near the mouth of Gleann Leac na Muidhe is forced through a narrow gorge and boils and thunders when there is a spate. There are also large rocks in the centre of the current. Could this have inspired the scene? Long ago I stopped worrying about a precise crossing and put it all down to Stevenson again, wisely using his imagination to develop the story and excite his readers.

It's the same with that great rock David and Allan climbed at dawn to hide from the soldiers. They lay there all day while the search went on below. It was a day of scorching sunshine, they had brandy but no water, and were left to 'birstle' on their rock, as Allan described it, like scones on a girdle. At the exit of Gleann Leac na Muidhe, there is a large heather-topped rock used in the making of one of the *Kidnapped* films, but in reality the fugitives would have been discovered there within minutes. The nearest that fits is Signal Rock, which stands high off the river and is unobserved unless from high on the flanks of Sgorr nam Fiannaidh. Almost certainly Signal Rock would have been pointed out to Stevenson on his visit as a local landmark. If Stevenson knew Meannarclach, then he also knew Signal Rock. Several people can hide on its flat top, and unless they show themselves, they are invisible from the glen below. Again there is no entirely satisfactory location, and none of my friends have fared better in their searches. Still, it creates further excitement:

> … we could see the soldiers pike their bayonets among the
> heather, which sent a cold thrill into my vitals; and they would
> sometimes hang about our rock, so that we scarce dared to
> breathe. It was in this way that I first heard the right English
> speech; one fellow as he went by actually clapping his hand on the
> sunny face of the rock on which we lay, and plucked it off again
> with an oath. "I tell you it's 'ot," says he.

But no written word, illustration or photograph can convey the sheer drama of the Glencoe landscape. I find it hard to stand on Signal Rock and take my eyes from that towering wall of Stob Coire nan Lochan, scoured by centuries of water courses, and the sharp chainsaw blade that is the ridge of the Aonach Eagach high on the left, with Clachaig Gully, longest and one of the most treacherous in Britain, gouging its side. Some people find Glencoe gloomy and depressing, as if the slaughter of those 37 MacDonalds there in 1689 had somehow sunk into the psyche. The historian, Lord Macaulay, called it the 'Glen of Weeping … melancholy, brooding, the very Valley of the Shadow of Death'. I have never found it so. From my climbing days, the sight of those big tops on a clear, starry night, especially in winter with the moon shining bright on the snow and ice, gave me a squirt of adrenaline and a turn of the stomach in anticipation of clambering up there

FIGURE 39. Signal Rock in Glencoe commands a view over the lower part of the glen. This local landmark would have been pointed out to Stevenson during the research for *Kidnapped*. The chances are that it was on top of this rock that Stevenson hid David and Allan, while the redcoat soldiers bayoneted the heather around them. The top is unobserved from below and is big enough to conceal several people. *Alun John*

next day. Maybe there was even a tinge of fear. I still find it hard to drag myself away from their company.

On Signal Rock I took stock of my day. It didn't bother me that I hadn't followed David and Allan's route exactly, because I don't think Robert Louis Stevenson was sure of it anyway. In any event, I knew Meannarclach well enough and I had been along the Aoneach Eagach several times in both directions. I had previously reached the summit of Bidean nam Bian, and once helped the Kinloss Mountain Rescue team bring down a seriously-injured climber avalanched off Fork Gully on Stob Coire nan Lochan. I felt I knew this section of the route at least as well as Allan Breck.

David and Allan had spent their day on the rock. I decided to spend the night in the wood around Signal Rock. Caolasnacoan and the Heugh of Coire na Ciche, where David and Allan went into hiding for a few days, was an easy if steep pull in the morning.

II

The Moor

How Allan Breck made a 'fiery cross' with the help of a sprig of birch, pine and his silver button, I sleep snug in the Heugh of Corrynakiegh, prove I am a dab hand at guddling, hear of a lost sheepdog, have an adventure with a poacher, and head out across the wilderness of Rannoch Moor.

'We'll wheech into the Heugh of Coire na Ciche for a guddle,' I said tongue-in-cheek to my friend Alun John, former picture editor of *The Independent* newspaper, who took many of the photographs in this book. Alun is a Welshman undiluted by years of living in the far south, and he looked totally bewildered. We were driving to various *Kidnapped* sites, camera at the ready, and approaching Caolasnacoan farm, where Allan Breck hid in the cleft on the hillside above. I translated that we would quickly turn into the farm, visit the site, then catch brown trout in the burn with our hands. That was what Allan Breck and David Balfour had done 250 years previously. Tasty, too, if lacking a pinch of salt, was David's verdict, and there are still trout splashing in that burn today.

I suddenly realised how Stevenson's editor must have felt when he first saw the *Kidnapped* manuscript. He had pointedly instructed Stevenson to ration the Scots words for the sake of his growing army of readers around the world. When he read 'The Heugh of Corrienakiegh' in a chapter heading, the poor man must have groaned. It was, however, the correctly-named location of Allan Breck's hideout.

After a night of peaceful slumber at Signal Rock in my 1960s time warp, I slogged up the steep slopes of Sgorr nam Fiannaidh, which marks the end of the Aonach Eagach ridge. My target was the Pap of Glencoe, or, to give it its proper name, Sgorr na Ciche, that

FIGURE 40. Allan and David guddled for brown trout and cooked them in the Heugh of Coire na Ciche above Caolasnacoan. All that was missing, they agreed, was a pinch of salt. Small trout still dart and splash in the burn. Today the author demonstrates that he has lost none of the guddling skills he learned in childhood. *Alun John*

knob of rock high above Glencoe village like an identifying fingerprint on every photograph taken in the area. The view from this rocky perch is stunning. I remember once reaching the Pap just before sunset after a summer traverse of the Aonach with a companion – and there was a shimmering pink Loch Linnhe below, a deep-purple Beinn a' Bheithir, a light-blue Ben More on Mull in the distance against a yellow-silver sea, and even the rocks around us were of red gold. The Ardgour hills were of hues unknown to man. We watched in silence until darkness began to take over. Even to cough could have broken the spell. We descended several hundred feet without a word and then only to murmur 'Say nothing'.

A burn known as the Allt Coire na Ciche gathers just below the Pap and tumbles steeply down its northern side, gathering volume and pace. As the burn descends, it cuts into the hillside, and rowans, birches, firs and alders fill its deep banks. It was in this wood that

Allan Breck hid after the shooting of Colin Campbell, a bolt-hole that was well chosen because he could see without being seen, and there were several escape routes at his back. Caolasnacoan farm in those days was near the lochside, so Allan Breck need not have placed himself high in the gully to be invisible. If the soldiers arrived, as they did after he took to the heather, he could have gained height from within the cleft without being observed.

Stevenson brought David Balfour and Allan Breck to the same hideout. It is indeed named the Heugh of Coire na Ciche, although RLS chose to make it one word instead of three and changed the spelling to Corrynakiegh, which may have been an old version. Here they made themselves at home, listened to the cushat-doves, whaups, cuckoos, admired the scenery and guddled trout from the burn. There are three 'caves' up there, but in reality more overhangs or holes in the fallen rock than proper caves, and nothing like the scene depicted in *Kidnapped*. It may be that Stevenson saw what looked like the black mouth of a cave high on the hill from the other side of the loch, and simply dangled it down a thousand feet into the Heugh to fit his purpose. Cushats are still there and the trout are not difficult to catch if you know the art of guddling.

My own guddling skills were learned as a boy in the Birnam burn near Dunkeld. The knack is not to be squeamish. Roll up your sleeves, better still, take off your shirt, and get down to the job. Feel into the nooks and crannies of the burn, under the rocks and stones, keep your eyes peeled for giveaway darting shadows. You will know when you touch a trout! Depending on the confined space below the stone, it will likely try to wriggle away. Follow it with your fingers, stroke it gently from below, move your hands slowly up to its gills. Once there, sink in your fingers! I caught three in half an hour, beautifully marked and shining, then gently returned them to their pool. For me even dramach tastes better than trout.

It was in the Heugh of Coire na Ciche that Allan borrowed his silver button from David, fashioned a cross, blackened the ends in the fire, and bound to it a sprig of birch and fir with a strip from his coat. This was to be his calling card at the house of John Breck Maccoll, the bouman who lived in the clachan of Caolasnacoan below. Allan explained: 'This cross is something in the nature of a crosstarrie, or fiery cross, which is the signal of gathering in our clans; yet he will know well enough the clan is not to rise, for there it is standing in his window, and no word with it. So he will say to himsel', *The clan is not to rise, but there is something.* Then he will see my button, and that was Duncan Stewart's. And then he will say to himsel', *The son of Duncan is in the heather, and has need of me* ... then John Breck will see the sprig of birch and sprig of pine; and he will say to himsel' ... *Allan will be lying in a wood which is of both pines and birches.* Then he will say to himsel', *That is not so very rife hereabout;* and then he will come and give us a lookup in Corrynakiegh. And if he does not, David, the devil may fly away with him, for what I care; for he will no be worth the salt to his porridge'.

'But would it not be simpler for you to write to him a few words in black-and-white?' asked David.

'And that is a very excellent observe, Mr Balfour of Shaws,' said Allan joshing, 'and it would certainly be much simpler for me to write to him, but it would be a sore job for John Breck to read it. He would have to go to school for two-three years; and it is possible we might be wearied waiting for him.'

In real life, Allan Breck and James Stewart in particular had no reason to thank the same John Breck Maccoll. It was the bouman's perjured evidence, given under duress, that helped to send James to the gallows.

I spent a snug night in the Heugh of Coire na Ciche. The cushats were indeed cooing, I heard whaups call in the morning, the burn was musical and I was greatly entertained by a family of wrens which had made their home under an overhang of the bank. Their brown nest of dead bracken, complete with roof, was stitched on to the earth below and perfectly camouflaged. For such a little bird it has a very loud voice, and it was the male bird's song that woke me in the morning.

I was searching for the cave when I met the Caolasnacoan farmer at the time, Colin Cameron, gathering sheep on the hillside. His march went right up to the top of the Aonach Eagach, surely one of the highest, steepest – and most dangerous – grazings in Scotland. Colin knew the hillside and the surrounding country as well as his own fireside. 'It can get really rough up there, summer or winter, and you just can't take chances,' he explained. 'I once lost a dog up there for 11 days. A miracle she survived. Jean was her name, and a right good dog, too. She simply got lost in the mist. When the mist comes down thick like that it also deadens sound and you have to get off the hill fast. It's too easy to take a header over a cliff or become disorientated. We found Jean on a difficult, dangerous ledge. We got her off by tempting her with bits of meat then nabbed her with a noose on a long bamboo pole and swung her over. Aye, I suppose we were risking our own lives – and Jean's – but we didn't much think of that at the time. Saving poor Jean was what counted.'

Nowadays, Caolasnacoan has been turned into a caravan park overlooking Loch Leven. It is run by Colin's widow, Patsy, an effervescent Fifer, friend and chief adviser to all the caravan people. She knows all about the Appin Murder and Allan Breck's hiding-place up above her head. The last time I saw Patsy a golden eagle stopped our conversation in mid-sentence. It soared out from the Aonach and found a perching place somewhere high in the Heugh of Coire na Ciche. 'That's maybe a lucky sign,' laughed Patsy. 'Maybe you'll track down the Appin Murderer yet!'

The next stage of the *Kidnapped* Trail had been on my mind from the beginning. It was out over Rannoch Moor, that great, bald, empty badland, the biggest, uninhabited wilderness in Britain, around 50 square miles of bleakness with as many grumpy moods as uncompromising faces. Rannoch Moor was no small undertaking. People have set out and never returned. Allan Breck prepared David for what it meant to take to the heather across the Moor: 'Ye maun lie bare and hard, and brook many an empty belly. Your bed shall be the moorcock's, and your life shall be like the hunted deer's, and ye shall sleep with your hand upon your weapons. Aye, man, ye shall taigle many a weary foot, or we get clear! I tell ye this at the start, for it's a life that I ken well. But if ye ask me what other chance ye have, I answer: Nane. Either take to the heather with me, or else hang'.

Rannoch Moor is heaven or a freezing hell depending on weather and season. It is both moor and mountain, gullies, rocks, lochs, marsh, black-crusted bog, dark-brown peaty pools, and at intervals the whitened skeletons of the ancient Caledonian Forest poke out like the bones of long-deceased clansmen. The Moor stretches as far as the eye can see. Schiehallion rises like a great pyramid on the horizon about 25 miles away, marking Loch Rannoch and the southern boundary. The great mass of Ben Alder blocks the exit eastwards by Loch Ericht, and Bridge of Orchy is roughly its westward frontier. It is a wild, dreich, desolate place, devoid of people, and perhaps it is my imagination, but even birdlife seems scarcer, the calls of curlew and the croak of hoodies fewer and more muted.

It was an undertaking daunting enough for two people rather than one, I considered at the time. When I first marched the *Kidnapped* Trail, however, Rannoch Moor had to be an adventure postponed. My climbing companion was schoolfriend Jim Seaton, who many years later went on to edit *The Scotsman*. We both worked on the old *Weekly Scotsman*, and it was not possible for us to be off work together, although we were jointly writing a series of articles. I did the first section of the *Kidnapped* Trail from Erraid to Caolasnacoan on my own, then stopped there to return to work and come back another day. As it turned out, the first time Jim and I crossed on the *Kidnapped* Trail was from the opposite direction – and we experienced Rannoch Moor baring its teeth.

When I returned to pick up the trail on my own, my priority was to try to work out a route across the Moor. I had two fixed points: David and Allan found their way to Cluny's Cage on Ben Alder and, in real life, I knew from James Stewart's trial, Allan Breck on his flight had stayed for a couple of days with his uncle, Allan Oig Cameron, at Ardlarach above Loch Rannoch. Stevenson's minute-scale map indicates the route taken by David and Allan was below the north side of the Aonach Eagach, striking over the west side of the loch that is the Blackwater Reservoir today, then making directly for Ben Alder west of Carn Dearg and possibly also Beinn Pharlagain towards Loch Ericht. Exactness suffers in RLS's reduced map because it carries so little detail and the pencil-thin line of their route could be miles away from an unmarked feature. There is no easy route that does not involve a long hike in rough and hostile country and I was mindful of my first crossing with Jim Seaton more or less following the Stevenson map in reverse.

On that occasion, we caught the train for Dalwhinnie, then set out along the north shore of Loch Ericht and spent the night in a half-fallen wood above the loch. It was October, in the rutting season, and red deer stags roared throughout the night and some crashed alarmingly near us. We stopped for lunch at the abandoned Ben Alder Cottage, wonderfully situated above Alder Bay, with Ben Alder high overhead but out of sight. We headed out across the Moor with the weather overcast but fine. North of Rannoch Station we debated whether we should continue for another ten miles or so to Glencoe, or spend a comfortable, draught-free night in the Rannoch Station waiting-room. We decided to push on in the knowledge that part of the Moor would be completed in darkness. That's how David Balfour and Allan Breck handled it, we thought, so we would have first-hand experience.

We didn't count on the sudden change of weather. It was harder going and slower in the dark than we anticipated. The wind rose and with it came autumn snow and rain squalls. At times our vision was restricted to a few yards. We crossed the Moor by shining our torches on the pylon wires above our heads to give us our direction, yet even then such were the conditions that sometimes we had to scout around to find the next pylon. Then the snow eased and in the distance we saw a gleam of light that turned out to be a window in Black Corries farmhouse. Soaked and frozen, with the wind still battering, we knocked on the startled farmer's door and asked if we could spend the night in his barn. He peered into the darkness and his dialogue was like a poor 'B' movie script: 'Where have you come from?' he asked, an incredulous note to his voice. 'Not from the MOOR!' The farmer, however, was deadly serious. With good reason, too. In his and our minds was the tragedy of a few years earlier when five members of the Glencoe Mountaineering Club of Glasgow decided to spend Hogmanay in Ben Alder Cottage. They came off the train at Corrour Station in reasonable weather. As they headed up the hill above the Uisge Labhair burn, they hit deep snow, the conditions deteriorated, the wind became gale force and in the end only one of the five survived.

When I picked up the *Kidnapped* trail again at Caolasnacoan on my own, it was the height of summer and the sun was high. The Moor was like a drowsy pussy cat, never a claw showing, the lochs and peat pools dazzling, and the distant mountains stood blue-grey and shimmering. Close up the colours of Rannoch Moor were pastel, with sharply con-trasting dark greens, browns, yellows and reds, and the bell heather was out fully in clumps of purple as I passed. In these conditions crossing the Moor was a wonderful and exhilarating experience.

I left the Heugh of Coire na Ciche and headed out over the bealach to the south of Garbh Bheinn. The breeze was gentle, in my face, and I had discovered that coming upwind tended to

FIGURE 41. 'Wheesht! Not a sound,' whispers Allan Breck in this artist's impression of dragoons sweeping Rannoch Moor in the hunt for the two fugitives. Historically, dragoons did search the Moor after the murder. All known escape routes were blocked by government troops, and even suspicious outgoing east-coast shipping was intercepted in the race to catch Allan Breck.
The Writers' Museum

catch wildlife napping. I slowly poked my nose over a ridge to look down on the open ground below and as I did so I heard a rifle shot just in front of me. As I looked over the edge I saw two men. They had obviously been lying prone and were getting to their feet as I peeped over the brow. One lifted his rifle from the ground. About 50 yards away was a red deer hind on its side, legs kicking as if it were still trying to run across the hillside. The man with the rifle ran forward, took aim and fired again. The kicking stopped. Then he saw me.

There was a very long pause. He called two words: 'Jack, company!' Looking directly at me he shouted: 'Bastard!' I said nothing. They took off down the hill, where they probably had a car parked. A minute later they were out of sight.

I walked over to the deer. At that moment I would have done anything to have given it back its life.

They were poachers, of course. This was poaching country all the way down to the Bridge of Orchy area and beyond and red deer was the quarry. Some poachers made quite a good thing out of selling the venison to hotels and individuals, but mostly they were there for the thrill and the kill and getting away with it if they could. Colin Cameron, the Caolasnacoan farmer, told me he lost up to 20 sheep a year to trigger-happy poachers. If there were no deer around, they sometimes turned their sights on any animal that moved.

I looked for a calf and was relieved to find nothing. There was nothing I could do. I left the dead deer and moved on. Maybe they would return later or perhaps they merely shrugged off the incident. For them there was always another day.

Having followed David and Allan's footsteps by the *Kidnapped* map in reverse, this time I decided I would try to take what I thought might be Allan Breck's route. I reckoned Allan would not take the risk of being sighted on the open Moor and would therefore keep to the high ground, which gave him escape options north and west into the mountains and even a little eastwards. My guess was that Allan might have approached Ben Alder from the hills on the south side of Loch Ossian, and I made Ben Alder Cottage bothy my planned overnight stop. I cut across the present West Highland Way, an important military section of road then, and along the line of the Blackwater Reservoir. Allan Breck would have wanted to slip through this area quickly because the military road direct from Fort William was well pounded.

After Colin Campbell's murder, the scale of the hunt for Allan Breck was Scotland-wide. The redcoats were out in numbers to block his escape. Ports were alerted, the sloop *Porcupine* was ordered to intercept outgoing east-coast shipping, Glencoe and Glen Etive were searched and heavily patrolled. Stevenson again was historically accurate in describing dragoons sweeping Rannoch Moor, but not lance-in-hand dragoons on dashing chargers as in the popular image. These redcoat horse-soldiers were more likely to be mounted on garron-type ponies, effective enough for the conditions. Some of the dragoons were probably based in Rannoch Barracks, at Bridge of Gaur, at the west end of Loch Rannoch. These tough little horses could relentlessly ride down a man once sighted. The task for Allan Breck was therefore not to be seen, which he achieved. As the dragoons from

FIGURE 42. Across Rannoch Moor. 'Your bed shall be the moorcock's, and your life shall be like the hunted deer's,' said Allan Breck to David as they took to the heather. The Moor remains a great, bald, empty badland, the biggest uninhabited wilderness in Britain. It has grumpy moods and in bad weather it is uncompromising. The picture shows the author in 1960 with a shoulder of Ben Alder heaving up through the mist.

Rannoch Barracks searched the Moor, he was already across and under their noses a mile or two away at Ardlarach.

There was a rumour that Ardshiel, the exiled chief of the Appin Stewarts, had returned to Scotland, and this was reflected in the warrant issued by the Sheriff of Perthshire for Allan Breck's arrest: 'Whereas there is information that Charles Stewart late of Ardshiele attainted for High Treason is lately Arrived in Scotland and is skulking within this country, and that Allan Stewart alias Breck in the ffrench Service is come over to enlist men contrary to Law, and is susspected Guilty of the murder of Colin Campbell of Glenure ffactor on the fforfeit Estate of Ardshiele & others; These are granting Warrant to the Officers of the shire to search for & apprehend the person of the said Charles Stewart and of the said Allan Stewart alias Breck and to Committ them to prison within the Tolbooth of Perth therein till they be liberate by due course of Law Given att Perth the 21st May 1752 years. Signed Ja. Erskine'.

The authorities expected Allan Breck to make for the east coast, a surreptitious route he had used previously. Two 'Allan Brecks' were arrested: one at Leith, who was taken to Edinburgh Castle; the other was interrogated in Carlisle after being picked up in Annan. Both were soon found to be innocents caught up in the hunt and set free. The chase after Allan Breck was pursued thoroughly, relentlessly and at speed.

Stevenson never crossed the Moor himself and probably exaggerated its scale and severity. In good weather, if you're sensibly equipped and play it safe, the Moor can be a deeply rewarding experience. The terrain is rough, landmarks tend to change shape quickly, sometimes they unexpectedly vanish, and it is wise to keep the map handy. In good weather, a compass may seem needless, but it remains reassuring aid. In the long ago, Rannoch Moor was gouged by the Ice Age, then the great Caledonian Forest swept over and it became the hunting ground of many wolves. Such a plague of wolves that spittals or hospices were built to give protection to travellers caught late on the road. Both forest and wolves vanished in the orgy of tree felling to feed the craving of the iron furnaces for charcoal in the eighteenth century, but also to build the military road and later the railway. The last few wolves in Scotland were possibly still struggling to survive as Allan Breck made his getaway, but it is unlikely he heard those long, lingering, chilling howls in the middle of the open Moor with no hiding place.

Apart from my encounter with the two poachers, my own second crossing was a delight, although it became windless and sultry around lunchtime and the hills began to lose their sharpness. Scratched in my diary notes it says 'Lunch: two boiled eggs and cheese. Where are all the birds?' I remember sitting on a rock just looking, listening, taking perspective and thinking the Rannoch Moor experience was as good as a brainwash any day. Its sheer scale cuts people down to size. I could have been a blade of grass in the vastness of it all, a microdot in space as if the Moor were an upside-down sky. I watched blue-bodied dragonflies pass like silent toy helicopters, bumble bees drone to their precarious home below a rock – and suddenly I was bitten by a cleg and the air was full of nipping, flying ants. Such is the Moor!

My plan was to hit the railway line south of Corrour Station. I had once walked part of this route in winter with another climber friend from those days called Sydney Odd en route to Luibeilt bothy below

the Grey Corries in Nevis country and I knew I would feel in home territory. I was looking forward to striking the railway because the ups and
downs of the Moor, the peat hags and detours to avoid unnecessary
climbing with my big pack, made me ready for that height of Rannoch
Moor diversion – watching the trains go by. More accurately, certainly
in those days, it was watching the train go by if you were lucky. There
were not so many and, to be honest, after several expeditions across the
Moor, such has been my timing I have only ever seen two. However,
there is no better excuse for a rest.

Rannoch Station, Corrour Station! Desert halts at the end of full-
stop roads that go nowhere. But what a task those intrepid railway
builders of old had in pushing the rails out across that vastness in all
weathers. Sometimes they found peat beds so deep that brushwood
had to be dug in along the tracks to provide firmness. In winter, axes
were needed to break the ice in burns so they could boil their billy-
cans. It produced a railway culture of Scots and Irish labourers living
strange, unnatural, harsh bothy lives – toil, sweat, freeze, slave hard,
play hard, drink hard, fight hard. Each section of new line laid became
a glorification, the whole Moor railway project a dedication. Yet at
night with work over, the wilderness outside the huts might be regaled
with a whisper of fiddle, melodion or a snatch of bothy ballad before
the wind caught and hurled those small notes across the Moor.

From Corrour Station there is a good road to the end of the
glittering Loch Ossian. I found red deer everywhere, some in no hurry
to get out of my way, staring at me curiously as I passed. 'Not venison
again!' might well have been the cry from those intrepid railway
builders at meal times. My route was up the Uisge Labhair burn
beyond Loch Ossian, roughly in the tracks of those luckless Glasgow
climbers who lost their lives in the blizzard. Then over trackless
ground on the hillside to strike the path that leads through the Bealach
Chumhainn. After that it was an easy trundle of four miles or so down
to Ben Alder Cottage on Loch Ericht, my target for the night.

You will not find finer country or more austere. Its scale,
remoteness, grandeur – and sheer hardness – is awesome. I didn't see
another person all day. All that, of course, will change with the restora-
tion of Corrour Lodge at the end of Loch Ossian into a contemporary
Victorian Gothic edifice, a modern vision of a grand house. It is also
likely to mean bad news for the deer.

FIGURE 43. Safe house for a climber. Remote Ben Alder Cottage beside Loch Ericht has been a treasured bothy for climbers and walkers for years. As bothies went in the 1960s, it had windows and a watertight roof and therefore was considered luxurious. The author used Ben Alder Cottage as a base for an unsuccessful search for Cluny's Cage, one of the hideouts of the MacPherson chief, who chose to stay in Scotland rather than go into exile after Culloden.

My hike was uneventful except for one brief episode. As I left Loch Ossian and picked my way upwards, the sky grew darker until it became angry indigo. I remember thinking – with just a little exaggeration – it was like midnight at teatime. I had heard thunder rolling and echoing around the hills in the afternoon and now I could see it was at last coming my way. There was no shelter up there and the air had become heavy and eerily still. The lightning flash when it came seemed to sizzle and crackle and light the gloom. I had my rucksack off almost as fast because I suddenly remembered its metal frame. A few seconds later came a crack of thunder that almost brought me to my knees. The downpour was torrential, and with the rain came a buffeting wind that made me hide behind a rock. Little springs and burns appeared all around me, gurgling and rushing. They might as well have gushed down the back of my neck for it was impossible to be more sodden. A few more hisses of lightning and thunderclaps followed, none as loud as the big one, the air began to clear, then freshen, and by the time I reached Ben Alder Cottage, nestling beside Loch Ericht, the sun was out and I was beginning to steam. That roar of thunder was the loudest I think I have ever experienced – and just goes to show you never know what Rannoch Moor might hurl at you next.

As the property advertisements might say, Ben Alder Cottage enjoys a magnificent situation on Alder Bay with spectacular views across the loch and surrounding country. It has two rooms, no water, no loo, no furniture and no long-term residents, at least in my memory. It is a safe house for climbers and walkers and over the years they have treated it well. Loch Ericht is deep and dark and somehow – at least for me – cheerless, but as climbers' derelict bothies went at that time, Ben Alder Cottage was the Ritz, and I had the place to myself. I quickly changed into my dry clothes and hung my dripping things outside. I had planned to gather windblown branches from the little wood on the far side of the bay to light the cottage fire, but the thunderstorm had raised the level of the Alder Burn to such a torrent that it was impossible to cross. No fire, I thought, and my coldly saturated clothes would be the same in the morning.

There was a small stock of food in the bothy: tea, sugar, some tins, including a syrup sponge and a half-used jar of raspberry jam. Suddenly I had an overwhelming desire for toast with the jam spread thick. But my circle of climbing friends in those days scoffed at the idea of carrying bread. Unwanted weight and an unnecessary luxury, they claimed, and I always agreed. In any event, the few provisions left in the bothy were always regarded as emergency rations and some poor climber might yet be glad of them. That night, alone in Ben Alder Cottage, I felt quite deprived of my toast and raspberry jam and had to settle for an extra handful of raisins instead.

David Balfour and Allan Breck, of course, stayed in some style and comfort on their visit to Ben Alder in Cluny's Cage, located somewhere, it is believed, on a flank of the mountain. The Cage was the home of Cluny MacPherson, that wily old Jacobite chieftain, who preferred to live the life of an outlaw rather than seek exile in France after Culloden. Cluny royally entertained Prince Charles Edward Stewart in the Cage when the Prince was on the run, and the badly wounded Lochiel also found refuge there. One glance at that vast mountainside told me that discovering Cluny's Cage, even if part of it still exists, would be a dedication. There are plenty of 'caves' on Ben Alder, mostly formed by tumbled rocks, and Cluny used several hideouts in the area. At a later date I returned to Ben Alder Cottage and spent almost five days looking for the Cage, but I could find nothing that remotely fitted the description. The Stevenson map indicated the Cage might have been a mile or two northwards along the lochside from Alder Bay, but it is unlikely RLS had knowledge of a specific location.

One old manuscript, understood to have been written around 10 years after the Prince's stay, tells how Cluny was so concerned about Lochiel's health that he wove the cage for him into a rockface beside a tree overlooking a 'lake' 12 miles long. 'The upper room served for salle à manger and bedchamber', read the account, 'while the lower served for a cave to contain liquors and other necessities. At the back was a proper hearth for cook and baiker and the face of the mountain had so much the colour and resemblance of smoke, no person could ever discover that there was either fire or habitation in the place.'

Whatever Cluny's Cage looked like, I have been unable to find it, and neither to my knowledge have any of my friends. It may be that the tree rotted away, a rockfall destroyed everything, or that simply it was located elsewhere, possibly even on the other side of Loch Ericht.

That evening I stood at the door of Ben Alder Cottage and gazed into the night. The loch still reflected light from the sky, but the clouds had gathered again and there was a feeling of rain in the air. I could hear the sound of many burns. Ben Alder heaved up darkly behind, its bulk hidden from the cottage. I remembered once climbing up there in winter with Sydney Odd and finding Ben Alder's great, flat top encrusted with thick green ice. It was almost impossible to stand against the wind, and even when kneeling its force sailed us across the summit, but we were glad for the conditions and laughed as we controlled our progress with our iceaxes. The thought gave me a shiver and I unrolled my sleeping bag.

David Balfour was miserable below Ben Alder. He was unwell, Allan Breck had lost his money to Cluny MacPherson at cards, the mist and rain and the desolation began to intimidate him. It's going to be David Balfour weather again tomorrow, I thought, as I heard the wind rise and the first raindrops strike the window. But Rannoch Moor was now behind me and that was a relief – and I fell asleep wondering what kind of climber brings a jar of raspberry jam on a mountaineering expedition.

12

Farewell on Gullane Sands

How the fugitives chose the high road by Glen Lyon, Glen Lochay and Glen Dochart, quarrelled in the rain, and took part in a duel by bagpipes. I find there are talented pipers still in Balquhidder, discover an Allan Breck bolthole in Stirling, and come to the end of my journey on an East Lothian beach.

I have never heard of wet clothes as a form of torture, but pulling on a sodden shirt after a night of blissful slumber makes the warm flesh shrink from contact. With that first chill shock on skin in Ben Alder Cottage my whole body cringed and I groaned loudly. But it is a fool's game to be without a set of dry clothes in such contrary country, the rain was steady outside, and I had a long way to tramp. I would rely on having a dry change at nightfall.

David and Allan Breck were taken across Loch Ericht by boat, which saved them a squelching mile or two. A hill track links the south side of Loch Ericht to Loch Rannoch, but I made a short detour by the former clachan of Ardlarach, where the real Allan Breck stayed for two days as he made his escape. The rain was incessant, the mist ghostly, and I could hardly see the far shore of Loch Rannoch. Cluny's chief scout put the fugitives over to a point near Finnart, about two miles along the loch's south side from Bridge of Gaur.

Rannoch Barracks were at Bridge of Gaur. In Allan and David's day, they were a redcoat outpost in bandit country. The site is now part of the Finnart estate and I could see the old location on my right as I passed over the river. Stevenson's map is firm here but dismisses this section of the *Kidnapped* journey in a few sentences: 'The gillie put us across Loch Rannoch in the dusk of the next day, and gave us his opinion of our best route. This was to get us up at once into the tops of the mountains: to go round by a circuit, turning the heads of Glen

Lyon, Glen Lochay, and Glen Dochart, and come down upon the Lowlands by Kippen and the upper waters of the Forth'. Allan preferred eastwards through the country of his friends, the Atholl Stewarts, but Cluny's scout had all the government forces at his fingertips, named and numbered, and Allan would have encountered more enemies than friends.

Stevenson plotted this route with a reason, but I could make neither head nor tail of it, unless it was simply to exhaust David Balfour for the sake of the story. If this was the intention, he succeeded admirably. To my knowledge, Stevenson did not set foot in this tangle of glens, high passes, perpendicular hillsides, rock, scree and moor – and five peaks all over 3,000ft. His description in *Kidnapped* amounts to under 20 words and the area is skimmed in a paragraph or two, yet to my mind this section is almost as physically challenging as clambering in the clouds above Glencoe – that is if you follow RLS's instructions literally to climb into 'the tops of the mountains'. This meant in that wild section west of Glen Lyon attacking those massive guardians of the wellheads of the Lyon, the Lochay and the Dochart – Beinn Creachan (3540ft), Beinn Achaladair (3288ft), Beinn an Dothaidh (3283ft), Beinn Dorain (3524ft) and Beinn Chaluim (3354ft). As for me, I was also carrying my home on my back.

These hills are high, wild and exposed, and it is little wonder it was a nightmare for David Balfour as he began to succumb to the constant downpour, his watery bed in the heather and the sheer toil of climbing these mountains. David gave no indication how long this stretch took, but I had previously climbed three of these big tops on separate occasions and they are not hills to be waltzed over quickly, particularly in poor weather. I began to think Stevenson had underestimated the scale and toughness here, which may have reflected his unfamiliarity with the area. The fugitives were still making for Kippen, yet such a curve westwards gave them no advantage.

I decided to follow their footsteps at a lower level with no option but to tote my heavy pack all the way. I would clamp down for the night, I thought, where I could. I left Loch Rannoch by a track that petered out west of Garbh Mheall. A steady haul took me to a point where I overlooked Loch an Daimh, or Giorra as the dam is increasingly known nowadays, where the loch was dancing to the raindrops. I knew these were big, green hills around me, but the mist had turned them into shades of dull grey wherever a looming shoulder showed itself. I headed straight up the Feith Thalain burn, steep and foaming, until I was above Loch Lyon, then descended to the rocky lochside by a place they call the Sheilings, where I again began to have second thoughts about the route.

My thinking was this: neither Giorra nor the dam of Loch Lyon was there in David Balfour's day, or Stevenson's either for that matter. If they are removed from the map and Stevenson's clues are followed, it's more or less a straight line from Loch Ericht to the head of Loch Dochart. Glen Lyon was well populated in the mid-eighteenth century, but this route southwards would still be across trackless country, much less arduous and more direct. I began to feel Stevenson's top-of-the-mountains route was unconvincing. The full line is also marked on the west side of the mountains, too close for comfort, I thought, to the old military road almost at the foot of Beinn Dorain. It is the route of the main Glencoe road today as well as the Fort William railway line, busy enough even then, and it was this road James Stewart travelled on horseback to Edinburgh shortly before the murder. One of his overnight stays was at nearby Luib. Then I began to think if it was my neck that might be stretched on the gallows I, too, would play it safe and hold to the high ground. Perhaps it was my big pack that was questioning the route, for it was reluctant to be carried so high, and Stevenson was probably right after all.

I backtracked a couple of miles so I could spend the night in the wood at the site of the Lubreoch dam. I knew this area well and soon located the root of a fallen tree, which created a dry patch on one side, almost like a cave, and I was able to wriggle in. I was far from comfortable, but I could change into my spare clothes and creep into my sleeping bag, and the rain was easing. At a much later date I returned to take advice about the route from Bob Bissett, the retired Glen Lyon gamekeeper, who lived in the little cottage dwarfed by the towering dam wall. Apart from his stalking skills, Bob was an amateur historian, raconteur and Glen Lyon character. It was as if the inside of his cottage had been beamed in from a past age: the doorknocker was a fox's head, a fox's brush hung by the door, deerskins and a wildcat pelt were on the floor, along with a Robert Burns carpet. I counted 14 clocks, all ticking or striking merrily at the correct time; swords, daggers, a bayonet and a gintrap decorated the place. A telescope and

FIGURE 44. The sun breaks through the clouds below Beinn Dorain. Today this poet's mountain towers above the West Highland Way between Tyndrum and Bridge of Orchy, but in the old days it was the route James Stewart of the Glen took on his road to Edinburgh to try to win legal support for the Appin tenants. James spent the night in nearby Luib, Allan and David took the high road in the rain, and the author had a soft bed for the night in the back of a friendly car at Auch.

binoculars lay handy. Robert Burns plates were on the wall and Bob was proud of his Burns library. He repaired clocks, made fiddles, and lamps from deer feet and stags' horns. And he made shoes, including a size 17 for a giant. That was the kind of man Bob Bissett was. Glen Lyon was his patch, and he claimed to have insider information on the Appin Murder.

'It was a daft route they took,' said Bob. 'But I can understand why they wanted to go high. They were like the deer. In summer ye never see them because they're all up high. There's thousands up there but the mountains swallow them. At the far end of the loch, there was a better route they could have taken: up what's called the Fionn a' Glinne burn, over the pass between Heasgarnich and Craig Mhor, then down the Badamhain burn and they would have come out at the same place at the head of Glen Lochay. It's hard country up there though, and without shelter there's no surprise David Balfour took ill living in the rain.

'Would ye like to know who shot Colin Campbell of Glenure?' Bob suddenly asked. 'I'll no give ye a name, but I'll put ye in the right direction. It was a Cameron.' He would say no more, but tapped his nose wisely.

I found the route hard going. A wind had sprung up in my face as I traversed the inside of that giant semi-circle, well above the roots of the mountains. All these hills are above the treeline, blizzard-exposed, rock just below the surface, some of it outcropping, making walking rough and arduous. But I felt I had to make at least one effort to go high and slogged my way to the bealach between Beinn an Dothaidh and Beinn Dorain. I had climbed both of these tops previously, and Beinn Dorain, in particular, stands magnificently above the old military road and today's railway line. The Gaelic poet Duncan Ban MacIntyre, who was born in Bridge of Orchy in the eighteenth century, wrote a poem in praise of the mountain, and, from below, Beinn Dorain indeed rises high in poetic symmetry. Reaching the summit, however, was a fair pech, and I decided there and then I would sleep that night somewhere at its foot.

I was in luck. I was joined on the summit by two hillwalkers from Glasgow – David Clelland and David Stark – who invited me home to their tent pitched near Auch. They were appalled at my sleeping rough, possibly even more so at my diet of cheese, dramach and

FIGURE 45. The grave of Rob Roy MacGregor and his family is in
Balquhidder churchyard. His two sons, Coll and Robin Oig, lie on his left side.
It was Robin Oig who took part in the duel by bagpipe with Allan Breck, while
David lay sick in the house of Duncan Dhu MacLaren. There is no mention of
Robin Oig's hanging, but the words inscribed on the headstone above them
could be a battlecry from the past: 'MacGregor despite them'. *Alun John*

raisins. They were living like princes for a few days from the city,
and I joined them for their evening fry-up, which included three
slices of black pudding and two eggs in my billycan. I spent the
night on the back seat of their car in great comfort, and listened
to one of the Davids play a medley of folksongs on the moothie
from his tent.

Next morning I headed up the Allt Coralan burn back into the
hills with the rocky flanks of Beinn a' Chaisteil on my left,
through Glen Coralan making for the gap between Beinn Chaluim on
my right and Creag Mhor on my left, the wellhead of Glen Lochay.
This was rough, tough, steep country, big peaks bristled in all directions, but I just took my time, stuck one foot in front of the other,
and rested my big pack frequently. I was travelling lower than David
Balfour and Allan Breck, and it became increasingly clear that those
who held to the high ground also held the advantage, but these big,

bare tops provide no hiding places and, once seen, they would find escape difficult. It was no wonder they travelled by night. Stevenson was right again.

As they emerged from that mass of mountains and glens, a new range, with Ben More at its head, faced them across the glen. David's heart must have sunk at the sight. The exact route is difficult to follow here because Stevenson's map gives no names other than Loch Rannoch, Glen Orchy and the general area of Balquhidder. Their route on the *Kidnapped* map appears to round Ben More and Stob Binnein, dragging across the Braes of Balquhidder above Loch Voil and into the village. I had lost a little faith in the Stevenson drawing office by this time and on the ground there were a number of other possible options. David and Allan were still headed for Kippen or Balfron at this stage. The ruined Maclaren house at Invernenty, west of Loch Doine, I considered might have been a further choice. This was familiar territory for me and I had previously undertaken a trial hike down the Inverlochlarig route by way of Ben More and Stob Binnein and simply walked into Balquhidder village along the road.

But Rob Roy MacGregor and his murderous son, Robin Oig, are buried in Balquhidder churchyard in the village and Robin, who has a role in *Kidnapped*, once lived at the foot of Kirkton Glen. The Kirkton burn runs through the village and the whole scene here closely resembles the Robin Oig episode in *Kidnapped*. Stevenson knew this area reasonably well and I wondered if he was up to his tricks again, moving parts of the landscape around to better tell his story. So a third option, and the one I decided to take on the march, ran more eastwards, across the River Dochart at the ford near the old quarries (where I spent the night), then striking over the Kirkton Pass from Ledcharrie, past Rob Roy's Putting Stone, to come down the Kirkton Glen, which seemed to tie in neatly with the *Kidnapped* storyline if not the map. This is also MacLaren country, and the clan's gathering place was Creag an Tuirc (crag of the boar) just above the church.

It was somewhere above Balquhidder that David and Allan quarrelled. I recollect when I first read this chapter as a child, I was utterly shocked. The two best friends in life, who had endured dangers and adventures together – and they fell out in that high, wild, desolate place, swords drawn against each other. David, of course, was

sickening for his grave, as he put it. Resentment toward Allan for
losing his money to Cluny filled his mind. He thought constantly of
going in a separate direction. David became distant, cold and silent.
At first Allan was taken aback, unaware of David's plight. He tried to
win round his friend, but his pride, too, began to assert itself and, in
the end, he resorted to little taunts and jibes. It came to a head amid
the desolation of those grim mountains in the rain. The scene is so
fraught and realistic, it is as if it had been previously enacted. Perhaps
it had – in that awful quarrel Stevenson had with his father in an
upstairs room in Edinburgh's Heriot Row. A different backdrop – the
canyons of Edinburgh's New Town Georgian elegance – but the same
anguish. Both RLS and his parents had been emotionally devastated
by the experience.

As David and Allan faced each other at swordpoint in that
bleak mountain desert, Allan threw down his sword in confusion –
and simultaneously all David's anger oozed away. David was sick,
and sorry and blank and wondering at himself. Pride was forgotten.
All he could do was whisper: 'Alan! if ye cannae help me, I must just die
here'.

Allan half carried David following a burn down into Balquhidder.
I had decided to make it the Kirkton Burn. Allan knocked at the first
door they reached, and by good fortune it was the home of a
Maclaren, long-standing friends of the Stewarts.

David spent almost a month recovering in Balquhidder, tended by
Mrs Maclaren and her husband, Duncan Dhu. Duncan was a great
lover of the bagpipes, like so many Highlanders at that time. By day
Allan hid in a hole on the Braes and slipped down to visit David
in darkness.

It was on one of these nights he came face to face with Robin Oig.
Immediately, their sword hilts swung round for action. But Duncan
Dhu calmed them, and eventually produced his pipes. What followed
was a duel by bagpipe and Allan, who was considered a fine piper, was
vanquished. It was a dramatic encounter, but Allan summed it up with
great magnanimity.

'Robin Oig,' he said, 'I am no fit to blow in the same kingdom with
ye. Body of me! ye have mair music in your sporran than I have in my
head! And though it sticks in my mind that I could maybe show ye
another of it with the cold steel, I warn ye beforehand – it'll no be fair!

It would go against my heart to haggle a man that can blow the pipes as you can.'

Robin Oig now sleeps on Rob Roy's left hand with his brother, Colin, in the family grave in that little Balquhidder churchyard. Rob Roy's wife Meren (Mary) lies to the right. Violent, desperate times marked the MacGregors' stepping upon Scotland's stage and they played their own role to the hilt, with Robin Oig the wild one. His hanging goes unmentioned. Visitors from across the world now come to gaze on their last resting place. In their day, Rob Roy and his MacGregor 'Children of the Mist' were the most persecuted clan in the Highlands and those visitors may ponder that message from the grave carved above their heads which still echoes their defiance with a snarl – 'MacGregor in spite of them'.

I have a friend in Balquhidder called Jim Crumley, a former newspaper colleague, climber, writer, novelist, poet, columnist, and probably the only full-time wildlife author left in Scotland. In recent times, I asked him if the piping tradition in Balquhidder was still secure. In other words, Jim, I said, who are the Robin Oigs of Balquhidder today? He thought for a moment, then replied mysteriously: 'Get yourself to the King's House Hotel next Friday at 8pm and I'll tell you'.

So I duly arrived at the King's House and stepped into the wee public bar. It was standing-room only with local folk. Among them was Jim Crumley and also Roger Sharp, a deerstalker with the Edinchip estate – and under Roger's arm was a set of bagpipes. Then I knew what was coming. Balquhidder was holding a ceilidh. Jim had his guitar. First up were three children to give us a blaw on their chanters, and very good they were, too, and deserved their applause. Then Roger struck up with 'Loch Duich', and with the first notes I knew he was in the Robin Oig tradition.

Balquhidder is home to around half-a-dozen pipers nowadays. Roger, I am told, is maybe a grace note or two above the rest, but he has a deerstalker friend who can also hit the heights on his day, and Neil MacArthur, the manager of the King's House, has been blowing and squeezing the bag for nearly 30 years. The three youngsters on their chanters are Neil's pupils. In ancient times, the MacCrimmons were the legendary piping dynasty to the MacLeods of Skye, but the MacArthurs were pipers to the Lords of the Isles. That wasn't yesterday, of course, and Neil does not claim a direct link, but it is good to see young Balquhidder in such capable hands. Robin Oig would surely have approved.

Balquhidder is on the edge of high mountains, forests, green valleys and the Lowlands, and Jim Crumley is out there every day observing the wildlife. He has held editorial executive positions on a number of leading newspapers, but he threw all that up to do what he enjoys most. Balquhidder offers him everything: eagles are out there, ospreys float into his vision, red kites sometimes, a multitude of small birds and animals from badgers to foxes, otters venture up the Leny, and pine martens have established themselves in the forests, which gives him enormous satisfaction. Even his beloved wild swans are within easy reach at Loch Lubnaig. Jim is an expert on swans, and would not want to be far from their presence.

When David Balfour was well enough to leave Balqhuhidder it was August, four months after the Appin Murder. The pair were in tatters, their money almost gone. Allan considered the hunt would have slackened and even the bridge at Stirling would be watched less closely. 'It's a chief interest in military affairs,' said Allan, 'to go where ye are least expected. Forth is our trouble; ye ken the saying, 'Forth bridles the wild Hielandman'. Well, if we seek to creep round about the head of that river and come down by Kippen or Balfron, it's just precisely there that they'll be looking to lay hands on us. But if we stave on straight to the auld Brig of Stirling, I'll lay my sword they let us pass unchallenged.'

The line of their travels here is uncomplicated. *Kidnapped* covers about 30 miles in almost as many words and Stevenson's directions are precise. David and Allan made their way to Strathyre and spent the night in the house of another Maclaren because this was Maclaren country. Today the Maclaren of Maclaren, the chief of the clan, still lives in Balquhidder. The pair set forth again at nightfall on another easy stage, as David put it, and lay in a heather bush in Uam Var, within view of a herd of deer. This may not be as hard going as previous sections, but it is nonetheless a long way to Stirling and it has to be walked. I spent the night in a wood behind Strathyre, with a fine, clear sky above and listened to the sounds of dusk: a roedeer barking, the clucking of a pheasant as it settled into a fir tree, a red grouse birry-mick-micking on the moor in the distance, and then the

FIGURE 46. 'Forth bridles the wild Hielandman' went the saying, and the old bridge of Stirling across the infant river was a main access route to the Lowlands. Allan felt it would go unguarded, and he and David crept down to it under cover of darkness. Unfortunately, an alert sentry was on guard, the route was barred to them and the pair had to strike eastwards on the wrong side of the ever-widening Firth. The old bridge is still used by pedestrians.

rustling and whispers as the night-shift took over. On previous occasions, I had difficulty in pinpointing Uam Var and once spent two fruitless days trying to find it close to Callander. It is, of course, Uamh Mor, an outrider of Uamh Bheag, farther out on the moor than I originally thought. For such an unpretentious hill it even receives a reference from Sir Walter Scott in *The Lady of the Lake*. A cleft near the top is called Rob Roy's Cattle Fank, presumably reflecting his rustling activities in the area.

David and Allan may have taken the high road, but Ben Vorlich and Stuc a' Chroin, the mountains directly above Strathyre, are old friends of mine and I had no intention of greeting them again with my big pack. I traversed the flank of Beinn Bhreac, then south from the farm whose name tests Scots accents – Arivurichardoch – and out to Uam Var. It is a good haul on to Allan Water and the place formerly called Kippendavie, an acknowledged Jacobite house in its day. There has been a change of name now and Kippendavie has disappeared from the maps, but it was well known to Stevenson. I didn't want to lie too close to Dunblane, so I spent the night in a wood near the Ardoch Burn, and this time listened to the owls, but also peewits and curlews on the moor when they should have been sleeping. The weather was dry again and so was I, and from Balquhidder onwards the country was softening.

Stevenson was on familiar ground. For many years, Bridge of Allan was a favourite family Stevenson holiday resort, a spa which it was hoped would do something beneficial for the health of both Louis and his mother. The Stevensons had a set holiday pattern: first stay at the Queen's or the Royal hotel for a week, then seek boarding accommodation. RLS was around two years of age when he first went to this 'Queen of Scottish Watering Places', as Gilbert Farie, the local chemist and publicist, hailed the little town. RLS made walking expeditions all around the area, up to Uam Var, the cave by Allan Water, to the island in the Forth where he brought David and Allan to hide before trying to cross Stirling Bridge. Unknowingly, at the time these *Kidnapped* references were dropping into place for later use, and also possibly for other works. The local doctor in Bridge of Allan, Alexander Paterson, for example, may have been the model for Dr Jekyll in *The Strange Case of Dr Jekyll and Mr Hyde*. Gilbert Farie (Stevenson persisted in calling him 'Fairy'), who had a deformity, was somewhat cruelly described by Stevenson as '... the hunchback druggist of Bridge of Allan ... a terror to me by day and haunted my dreams at night ...' Farie could have developed into his frightening Mr Hyde.

David and Allan made their way down the Allan Water to where it falls into the Forth. There they found the little islet of Stevenson's childhood, overgrown with burdock, butterbur and other plants high enough to give them cover. As darkness fell, they headed for the narrow old bridge, with its twin pinnacles at each end. It is still a handy short-cut today for on-foot local folk over the infant Forth. The bridge at Stirling was the door of salvation for both of them, as David put it. He was for pushing straight over, but Allan was more wary. They waited.

Presently, an old woman with a crutch hobbled across. Then 'Who goes?' cried a voice, and the butt of a musket rattled on the stones.

'This'll never do', whispered Allan. 'This'll never, never do for us, David.' And without another word, he began to crawl away through the fields; and a little after, being well out of eyeshot, got to his feet again, and struck along the road that led eastwards.

In real life, Allan Breck's visit to Stirling may well have been of somewhat longer duration. From the moment of that last sighting at Innerhadden in Rannoch there has been mystery about his whereabouts. The next time he surfaced was in France some ten months later. So where had Allan Breck been? Who hid him? Stirling could hold the answer.

It is interesting to note that Stevenson was not the first to write a novel around Allan Breck. First was Stirling man George Robert Gleig, a soldier and military historian, who took holy orders and rose to become the British Army's chaplain-general. His novel, entitled simply *Allan Breck*, was published in 1834. It is entirely possible that George Gleig had considerable insider knowledge about his hero. More specifically, he may have known Allan Breck's whereabouts after the Appin Murder. Gleig's father was Bishop Robert Gleig, who had been the Episcopal vicar at Stirling. Among his Stirling flock were a number of families with strong Jacobite connections, including a direct link to Appin.

James Stewart was also a devout Episcopalian, a member of a church persecuted by the Hanoverians. When James visited Edinburgh early in April, 1752, as he tried to harness the law to work on behalf of the harassed Appin tenants, he stopped over in Stirling to consult a number of these families. Among them were William Wilsone of Murrayshall and his three spinster daughters. The daughters were recognised characters in the area for many years, who did not give a jot about hiding their Jacobite leanings at a time when it would have been more circumspect to keep quiet. Indeed, whenever the Hanoverian government was mentioned in church, the sisters shut their bibles with three distinct thumps and glared at the minister. It was hardly surprising, for their Aunt Isobel was the wife of Charles Stewart of Ardshiel, the same exiled leader of the Appin Stewarts and Colonel of the Appin Regiment who was hunted so sorely after Culloden. By his side throughout that harrowing period, of course, was Allan Breck. It is inconceivable the Misses Wilsone of Murrayshall did not know of

FIGURE 47. The foreshore at Carriden, near Bo'ness, where David and Allan
Breck were set ashore after being rowed across the Forth from Limekilns on the
Fife side. Carriden shore today has been industrialised, and as David walked
eastwards to South Queensferry he could never have envisaged today's giant rail
and road bridges spanning the river.

Allan Breck. For his loyalty to their uncle, he would surely be a
welcome visitor to their house at any time.

Now here is the twist. In his novel, George Robert Gleig has Allan
Breck hidden by three spinster sisters with Jacobite sympathies in a
lonely mansion near Stirling. Was he in the know? Did the Misses
Wilsone of Murrayshall really conceal Allan Breck after the murder or
pass him on to one of their friends? Was it arranged in advance? Does
it cast fresh doubt on James Stewart's innocence? After all, about five
weeks after James's visit to Stirling, Colin Campbell was dead and
Allan Breck had vanished. Did Allan Breck spend those unaccounted
months in the comfort of a Stirling safe house? If this were the case,
it would clear up a number of points in the mystery – but also set the
hares running again.

By the time Stevenson reached Stirling in the writing of *Kidnapped*,
his energy was faltering. He had been ill again and felt quite 'written

out' with exhaustion as he described it. He had already decided on the sequel, and in his mind *Kidnapped* was winding up. Perhaps he found the softer, lower country of the Carse of Stirling, beautiful as it is, did not have the same magic for him as the Highland sections. Whatever the reason, Stevenson fairly flew over the 25 miles or so on the north side of the Carse towards David's journey's end.

After the scare at Stirling Bridge, David and Allan sought less frequented parts again under the high line of the Ochils, as Stevenson decreed, by Alloa, Clackmannan, down to the shore of the Forth at Culross, and on into Limekilns. It is a long hike, but it takes Stevenson about 50 words with no description, and it gave me little pleasure for there were no clear guidelines, I had to climb fences, reason with a farmer, pacify barking sheepdogs, take avoiding action round a large white bull, and negotiate lethal roads.

Limekilns, however, is one of those north-bank village gems of the Forth, a mile or two westwards of the Forth Bridge. The Old Ship Inn on the waterfront is historically its senior pub, although it is unlikely to be on the same site as the *Kidnapped* change house. The Old Ship Inn was operating in Stevenson's time and he probably enjoyed a glass there. It continues as a local hostelry today. Alison Hastie was the 'bonnie servant lass', although you have to read *Catriona* to discover her name. Allan shamelessly 'chatted her up', as they say, and used poor David in his rags as an object of pity, hinting darkly that he was 'gentry' in the shadow of the noose. This was close to the truth and slowly they won Alison's trust. Apart from giving David and Allan a complimentary bottle of strong ale and a sympathetic free meal of white puddings, Alison Hastie agreed to row them across the Forth.

Now this is a feat that has always sounded false to me. To stand at Limekilns and look over the estuary, about two miles wide at this point, feel the buffet of even a gentle breeze, and stare out to the far shore at Carriden, to jump into a boat and start rowing is preposterous. And then Alison had to row all the way back to Limekilns. I put the thought to the test in recent times, with the present barmaid in the Old Ship Inn, young Hayley McCrindle, who in looks and age, I thought, could be another Alison Hastie. We stood on the seafront outside the inn and I explained Alison's Olympian row. Her

FIGURE 48. The beginning and end of David Balfour's wanderings ... it was from South Queensferry that David Balfour was kidnapped and it was here he returned to meet the lawyer Rankeillor and claim his inheritance. The old part of the town retains its antiquity, and even today, as David remembered, 'the smell of the sea water is exceedingly salt and stirring'.

assessment took a split-second. 'No chance!' said Hayley. 'I wouldn't try it.' And neither would I, Hayley!

I had an amusing experience in Limekilns when BBC presenter Lesley Riddoch and I made a radio programme about *Kidnapped*. To add a pinch of authenticity, producer Dave Batchelor insisted we also try to hitch a lift across the Forth. Fat chance, I thought to myself, even with Lesley's powers of persuasion, but we arrived at Limekilns mid-morning and made our way to the little harbour. The second person we asked was a yachtsman preparing to go out. Lesley was over to him in a flash with some story that the redcoats were hard on our heels, we were enacting the final scenes from *Kidnapped*, and could he please give us a lift across the river? To my great astonishment the yachtsman said: 'I know all about *Kidnapped*. Of course, I'll give you a lift. Where would you like to go?'

I couldn't believe it! Then I looked closer and under the nautical hat I recognised a friendly face from my past. It was old journalist colleague Gerry Grandison, whom I hadn't seen for at least 12 years. It was exactly the kind of thing he would do. He and his pal Colin Mackenzie took us over to the Hawes Inn. It was the maiden voyage of his yacht *Seapad*, and we spliced the mainbrace half-way over. Gerry believes that for those who know the currents in the Firth, rowing over would not be a difficult task. Stevenson also canoed in the river in these parts and knew what he was talking about, so between Gerry Grandison and Robert Louis Stevenson I humbly bow to their expert knowledge. Still, I wouldn't attempt it.

In *Kidnapped*, David and Allan were set down around Carriden near Bo'ness. The waterfront there nowadays is industrialised, the walking difficult, until Blackness Castle, where there is then a pleasant stroll into South Queensferry. It was almost the end of the journey. At the Ferry, David at last met up with his lawyer, Rankeillor. He walked into his house a penniless tramp and out again in smart borrowed clothes and with his future assured. Allan Breck had one last role to play. He confronted bad, old Uncle Ebenezer at the House of Shaws. For a moment the old swashbuckling Allan flourished once more and in top form. To a prevaricating Ebenezer he brought discussion to an abrupt halt. 'Come, sir, I would have ye ken I am a gentleman; I bear a king's name; I am nae rider to kick my shanks at your hall door.

Either give me an answer in civility, and that out of hand; or by the top of Glencoe I will ram three feet of iron through your vitals.'

The parting between David and Allan at the Rest-and-be-Thankful on Edinburgh's Corstorphine Hill was hard when it came. They made their plans and in silence looked over the fields and woodlands to the Old Town clinging to its defensive ridge. In those days, the New Town of Edinburgh was still only an idea, although it is interesting to note that the famous 'Proposals', which changed the face of the Capital, were published in the same year as the Appin Murder.

'Well, good-bye,' said Allan and held out his left hand. 'Good-bye,' said David and gave it a little clasp. That was it. After all their adventures together, they went their separate ways with never a backwards glance. As David said, however, once out of sight he felt like sitting down by the dyke and weeping like a child.

That sad parting caught the imagination of the brewers Scottish and Newcastle, whose headquarters on Ellersly Road is near the scene. They commissioned Scottish classical sculptor Alexander 'Sandy' Stoddart to create David and Allan in larger-than-life size to stand for ever looking out towards the Pentland Hills. Sandy Stoddart's magnificent bronzes, with such attention to historical detail in such a setting, bring them to life in a manner and understanding that would have delighted Robert Louis Stevenson.

But it would be a pity to leave it there. I have always felt *Kidnapped* had something of a sawn-off ending, almost an anti-climax. Stevenson strongly hinted, of course, that David and Allan would meet again for further adventures. The end of *Kidnapped*, therefore, was the beginning of *Catriona*, with Allan hiding in a haystack down at Silvermills, before David joined him on a last, desperate march, which turned into a frantic dash towards North Berwick. A boat waited behind the little island of Fidra to take Allan off to France and safety at last. North Berwick was also Stevenson country, and his East Lothian touch here is certain and assured.

Stevenson wrote *Catriona* in Samoa and those familiar Edinburgh names were remembered fondly as he set them down. David and Allan headed for the Gullane Sands by moonlight. Through Broughton and Picardy they walked, still villages then; a light in an upper window guided them silently through Lochend, then it was by the muir and bog of the Figgate Whins, where they lay under a bush till dawn about five. Haddock breakfasts were at Musselburgh and Allan, still wearing that same French greatcoat he retrieved from James Stewart's home in Acharn, began to suffer in the warm weather. From Prestonpans they made their way to Gladsmuir, where the perspiring Allan insisted they spend a few minutes just to give David a flavour of that famous Jacobite victory. They found Cockenzie a back-going town, although herring busses were being built at Mrs Cadell's, but the ale-house was clean and Allan indulged in a bottle to slake his thirst. It was there they saw one of their pursuers, and the pace became almost a run.

'Have ye seen a horse?' Allan gasped twice as they came upon country folk. It was always best, he explained, that for 'them that cannae tell the truth should be aye mindful to leave an honest, handy lee'. They struck the Gullane Sands near Dirleton, and suddenly there was the sea and that string of islets – Craigleith, the Lamb and Fidra – standing sharp and clear. Stevenson walked that shore many times. Every time I wander along that same beach it is a joy, and in my mind's eye I see Allan and David emerging from the bents, Allan wading into the sea to be picked up by Andy Scougal in his skiff and rowed out to the waiting *Thistle*. David was left forlorn on the beach to be kidnapped for the second time, taken out to the Bass Rock to prevent his giving evidence at James Stewart's trial. 'Black Andie' Dale, a local man, was David's captor on the Bass, along with James More's silent Highlanders.

Andy Dale and Andy Scougal? The farming Dale family were Stevenson's cousins and still continue to farm in the area. Andy Scougal took his name from the Dale's Scoughall Farm (pronounced 'Skole'), four miles along the coast eastwards from North Berwick, and a fine, productive farm it remains today. To bring the Dale and Robert Louis Stevenson connection up to modern times, Anne Dale married George Gray, another of those well-known East Lothian farming families. Much later, fittingly, Anne became chairman of the Robert Louis Stevenson Club, with its far-flung membership around the world.

The beach and rocks below Tantallon Castle are Dale country, near St Baldred's Cave, and the secret cove, where smugglers brought their contraband. It was a favourite spot for Stevenson, visiting his cousins, facing the mysterious Bass rearing out of the sea only a couple of musket shots away, on a coast that was a ships' graveyard for centuries, a haunt of pirates in the old days. Such a place in such surroundings was special for Stevenson. It is also a special place for Anne Gray and her family today, where they picnic with friends on that same beach where Stevenson strolled.

It was there on the shore that I came to the end of my own wanderings. They had taken me 40 years and I calculated about 300 miles from Mull to Gullane Sands and the black rocks below Tantallon Castle. Then there were all those months of pleasant detective work, in reference rooms from Edinburgh, London, San Francisco, Samoa and even Sydney, which I found almost as exciting as the discovery of Balfour's Bay on Erraid or the spot where that assassin lay in wait for Colin Campbell when I first marched the *Kidnapped* Trail. Robert Louis Stevenson still has a knack of opening doors that to some writers might remain closed, and he has certainly introduced me to many of his friends wherever I have gone. Stevenson used to be required reading in Scottish schools – along with Burns and Scott – but sadly that is no longer the case, although stage, radio and television producers and film-makers still find Stevenson and his works popular with their audiences. It is to be hoped Scottish educationists will think again about teaching Scottish children more about the great Scottish writers and poets.

I believe there is still a mountain of knowledge about Stevenson to be found out there, at least as high as Ben Alder, and about Allan Breck and Scotland's story, too, for that matter, with perhaps an adventure or two to be experienced in its finding ...

Postscript:

The Stewart Secret

Who fired the shot that killed Colin Campbell of Glenure in the Wood of Lettermore?

As someone who has tried to cast light on both Stevenson and the Appin Murder for many years, how much closer have I come to finding out the name of the Appin assassin? And is the secret name really being handed down after 250 years?

The answer is, yes, the name is being handed down. Unquestionably. Probably about 20 people know the secret. I know the names of seven of them.

Should the name now be revealed? Does it matter any more? Does anyone now care? The answer is that it most certainly matters to those Stewarts who know the secret – and they care passionately.

If I knew the name, would I tell? The answer is no, I would not now tell. Strangely, I set out all those years ago to discover the truth, but the more I have understood, the more I have felt it is not my secret to give away. Do I know the name? The answer is no – although I might.

I have now come to regard the name of Glenure's assassin as a private Stewart secret – and I respect their right to keep it private. In an age when privacy tends to be given short shrift and 'secrets' are revealed almost daily in headlines, the Stewarts have retained their secret for two-and-a-half centuries. It is therefore not to be given away lightly or cheaply. It is for Stewarts only to reveal when and if they want. Or not at all.

If it were a Campbell and not a Stewart mystery, the view would be the same. If it were a Campbell secret, the Campbells would also remain silent. That is the clan way.

The closer I have come to the Appin assassin, the more I have felt an outsider in what is essentially clan business. What has surprised me over the years is how in some senior clan circles the feuds, suspicions and rivalries of old have never entirely been put aside. In spite of denials and claims that claymores are buried and all is now friendship, the old clan loyalties and enmities are just below the surface. In those senior clan circles, clan tradition, history, integrity, honour – those very qualities which tend to be dismissed today – remain important.

What about poor Seumas a' Ghlinne, James Stewart of the Glen? Was he hanged an innocent victim or was he guilty of complicity as charged? This, of course, is another Stewart 'secret'. All my researches and private discussions indicate that James was innocent. His execution was a miscarriage of justice.

What about Allan Breck? Clearly Allan Breck knew something, but the weight of circumstance suggests he may not have been the person who pulled the trigger.

The Dewar Manuscript's folktale points the finger directly at Donald Stewart of Ballachulish as being the assassin. There is not enough evidence to know for certain that he or his brother John were involved or if there really was a Stewart gentry plot. If Donald Stewart was involved in a plot, then the tracks were cleverly covered.

There will be other future writings on the Appin Murder and more facts in time will be revealed. In the words of James Stewart's defence lawyer, the murder was 'the foulest and most barbarous that has occurred in any country'. An honourable man doing a difficult task was gunned down and an innocent man paid with his life. But until a Stewart decides to tell what really happened in the Wood of Lettermore, perhaps the Appin Murder mystery is now like the Loch Ness Monster up the road – better for everyone if it is never solved.

Index